I0132037

Edith Carpenter

Your Money or your Life

Edith Carpenter

Your Money or your Life

ISBN/EAN: 9783743303775

Manufactured in Europe, USA, Canada, Australia, Japa

Cover: Foto ©Thomas Meinert / pixelio.de

Manufactured and distributed by brebook publishing software
(www.brebook.com)

Edith Carpenter

Your Money or your Life

YOUR MONEY OR YOUR LIFE

SCRIBNER'S POPULAR SERIES OF

Each
12mo
COPYRIGHT NOVELS
75
Cents

WILLIAM WALDORF ASTOR . VALENTINO: AN HISTORICAL ROMANCE
ARLO BATES . . . . A WHEEL OF FIRE
H. H. BOYESEN . . . . FALCONBERG
MRS. BURNETT . . . . THAT LASS O' LOWRIE'S
"   "   . . . . . VAGABONDIA: A LOVE STORY
G. W. CABLE . . . . JOHN MARCH, SOUTHERNER
EDITH CARPENTER . . . . . YOUR MONEY OR YOUR LIFE
EDWARD EGGLESTON . . . . . . THE CIRCUIT RIDER
HAROLD FREDERIC . . . . . . THE LAWTON GIRL
ROBERT GRANT . . . . FACE TO FACE
MARION HARLAND . . JUDITH: A CHRONICLE OF OLD VIRGINIA
JOEL CHANDLER HARRIS . . FREE JOE AND OTHER SKETCHES
JULIAN HAWTHORNE . . . . . . A FOOL OF NATURE
J. G. HOLLAND . . . SEVENOAKS: A STORY OF TO-DAY
"   "   . . THE BAY PATH: A TALE OF COLONIAL LIFE
"   "   . . ARTHUR BONNICASTLE: AN AMERICAN STORY
"   "   . . . . . . MISS GILBERT'S CAREER
"   "   . . . . NICHOLAS MINTURN
COM'R J. D. J. KELLEY . . . . . A DESPERATE CHANCE
G. P. LATHROP . . . . . . AN ECHO OF PASSION
JULIA MAGRUDER . . . . . . ACROSS THE CHASM
BRANDER MATTHEWS . . . . . THE LAST MEETING
DONALD G. MITCHELL . . . . DREAM LIFE
"   "   . . . . . REVERIES OF A BACHELOR
HOWARD PYLE . . . . WITHIN THE CAPES
"Q" (A. T. QUILLER-COUCH) . . THE SPLENDID SPUR
"   "   "   . . THE DELECTABLE DUCHY
R. L. STEVENSON . . . . THE EBB-TIDE
"   "   . . . . TREASURE ISLAND
"   "   . . . . . . THE WRONG BOX
F. J. STIMSON . . . . GUERNDALE
FRANK R. STOCKTON . . . . . RUDDER GRANGE
"   "   . . . . . THE LADY OR THE TIGER

YOUR MONEY OR YOUR LIFE

A STORY

BY

EDITH CARPENTER

CHARLES SCRIBNER'S SONS

NEW YORK 1899

CONTENTS

NOTE

"Your Money or Your Life" obtained the prize of $1,000 in the story competition instituted by *The New York Herald* in 1895

YOUR MONEY OR YOUR LIFE

CHAPTER I

MUTINY

Tom Norrie sat at his desk in the great office, with his hands thrust deep in his pockets and his eyes lost in space. All about him men were hard at work, trying to clear off the accumulations of the day in the brief hours left before the day should end. The office boys ran to and fro, and the typewriter girls were rattling their machines as if on a race for a stake. Through the whole great room sounded the murmurous hum of work — the scratching of pens, the rustling of paper, the low consultations between one clerk and another, the slamming together of the big books on the bookkeepers' desks, the steady reiteration of the stamping-machines putting their hall-marks on the checks and bills and letters of the day.

In at the windows, flung wide to ease the oppressive heat, came the reverberant noises of the street, increasing thunderously to drown the lesser murmur of the office as some heavy brewer's dray went pounding by, then lulled to a momentary, low drone, above which could be heard each movement within. Across the street the brick buildings were blinding in the full sunshine, and men passed in their white shirt-sleeves, puffing, and mopping their faces. Yet the glare and dust and heat were not those of midsummer ; even in the heart of the city the breeze that now and then fluttered through the windows, making a quick stir over all the desks, and cooling the hot heads of toiling clerks, brought with it the breath of spring, almost an odor of the fields and woods, a moving suggestion of new life and vigor and gladness.

Tom Norrie's desk was a confusion of loose papers — the letters of the morning, with their typewritten answers now waiting his approval, bills and orders to be passed upon, a small pile of checks to be signed, plans and specifications for the new factories to be gone through, a hundred matters that pressed for his speedy notice. His was that orderly business habit that tolerated no postponement. One day's work put off until another kept him awake at night and gave him a feverish impetus wherewith to put twelve hours' work into the next day's nine. Many things had worried him of late, but nothing worried him so much as ragged edges of unfinished business. He made in his thoughts, instinctively, a picture of each day, as it passed, and the pictures of those days when he did not do all that was brought him to do were like untidy rooms, comfortless and dismal, or like a shiftless garden where the peas slopped into the beans, and the beans trailed into the strawberries, and weeds grew everywhere. He took charge himself of the garden at the family country place—a garden concealed by hedges and vine-covered trellises, and divided into the most exact of rectangular beds, with the straightest of neat paths between. Many unfortunate gardeners and gardeners' boys had been parted with because their conceptions of their art placed the welfare of the garden's contents above the perfectness of the garden's form. But to Tom Norrie order had come to be more than the heart of the matter, whether in horticulture or business, and in his grinding at detail he had lost his larger sense of the plan.

Yet to-day his desk lay piled with papers, and he sat inert before it, with his hands in his pockets. It was long after three. An office boy brought more papers and laid them before him, and looked at him with round eyes of astonishment. The afternoon mail was placed upon his desk, but appeared to concern him not at all. When the breeze came in he sniffed it absently, and this was the only sign of life he gave. The clerks near by began to look at him, and then at each other furtively, with little smiles. Their young chief had gone out at eleven, and had not come back until after two ; yet in the hour or more since that he had sat there at his desk, with various important matters delayed till he should give them his notice, he had not lifted a hand to his work. They looked in through the glass walls of the private office, where sat the two senior part- ners, and wondered when this curious aber- ration would receive its fitting attention from headquarters.

Tom Norrie sniffed the breeze, and pres- ently, catching an odor foreign to it, he too turned his head—he had not stirred before for an hour—and looked into that inner sanctum. His father, a pale, spare man, nervous, yet silent, was bending busily over his desk with his back towards the office. The other partner was stout, but very tall, with heavy black hair and mustache and a scowling brow—a physical make-up that fully justified the nickname of "Bull," by which he was known to his subordinates. His name, besides, was Trumbull, and his function in the partnership was to originate all new schemes, and to increase the already enormous business as much as the cautious conservatism of his partner, the "Bear," would permit. The Bull had just taken off his thin office coat and with his red face in high contrast to his white shirt-sleeves, sat smoking a cigar for the relief of his overheated bulk. Tom Norrie, too, liked a cigar, but it was one of the rules of the office that no smoking should be done outside the glass partition. For four years now he had been a partner, yet still was given no more liberty than when he first entered the office, a boy of twenty-one. The Bull and the Bear were both autocrats in the first degree, their difference being that one was a blustering, progressive autocrat, and the other a quiet, retrogres-

sive one. The unlikeness of their methods
was followed by perfect likeness in results—
neither was ever disobeyed. The clerks in
the employ of Norrie, Trumbull & Co., one
or two of them now men of fifty and sixty,
lived a life of terror and suppression, and
were treated like insubordinate boys in a
boarding-school. They all derived some
comfort from the fact that Thomas Norris,
Jr., was no better off than they, and looked
on with discreet pleasure when now and
then he fell foul of the authorities and met at
their hands his merited chastisement.

But to-day, when the young man had
sniffed for a moment the pleasing odor of
the Bull's excellent cigar, he drew one from
his own pocket and calmly lit it. As he
smoked he resumed his contemplations, and
the office, thrilled with excitement by his
foolhardy act, was obliged to keep at work
when that act was followed only by calm.
Yet those whose desks were nearest the private room soon became aware of signs of uneasiness within, and this significant fact was
quickly transmitted from one to another by
meaning flashes of the eye. The Bull was
roused at last. He saw Tom's cigar, he saw
his heaped-up desk, he saw the young man's

hands in his pockets. The atmosphere of the office became, as it were, charged with nervous anticipation of the upheaval to follow, but Tom smoked on, all unconscious, apparently, of these electric omens in the air. Presently the Bull rose and stalking forth from his fastness stopped at Tom's desk. Tom, tilted back in his chair, did not change his position nor remove his hands from his pockets, but regarded Mr. Trumbull's frowning face with perfect serenity.

"Are you going to have time this afternoon to see the Slosson Company about their orders?" growled the elder man.

"No, I don't think I am," replied Tom, sweetly. He looked straight in the Bull's face with a pleasant smile.

"It's the most serious affair you've got on hand. While you're twirling your thumbs Roberts will get in ahead and get the orders."

"I'm in no hurry," said Tom. "I'm willing Roberts should get the orders if he wants them—I've something more important to do," he added after a moment.

"You'd better be about it then." The Bull's voice had an ominous sound.

"I'm going to when I've finished my cigar," returned Tom, tranquilly. "Hot day, isn't it? Good day to get into the country."

The Bull said nothing. He merely glared at Tom with an expression that suggested biting his head off. Then he went across the room, by rows of trembling clerks, who bent busily over their desks as he passed, and blew up the head bookkeeper, until the whole office turned pale and the smoke of warfare was almost visible. As he returned, his face redder than ever, he looked again at Tom's desk.

"Merriam," he called out to a man near the back of the room, "come over here and do Mr. Norrie's work for him. He has something more important to do."

"Oh, thanks," said Tom, urbanely, while Merriam rose and stood hesitating. "That's very kind, Mr. Trumbull. It would be a convenience to have Merriam do my work this afternoon. I've got to go out in a minute."

Merriam came and stood by his desk.

"Just wait a minute," said Tom, and with the Bull still glaring at him from the door of the private office, he pushed the papers before him aside, leaned forward, and wrote a brief note. He rose as he finished it, put it in his pocket, and flung away his cigar. "You'll find plenty to do there, Merriam," he said to the old confidential clerk, who stood pale and patient, looking down at the cluttered papers. "You'd better have Atchison leave his estimates and help you, or it'll take you all night."

The young man took his hat from the rack and went into the private office. The Bull stood by his desk, his face like a thunder-cloud, but Tom had the air of not seeing him. "Just tell the girls not to expect me to-night, will you, father?" he said. "I'm not going home." His father, who had been too busy to take in the events of the previous ten minutes, looked up in surprise.

"Where are you bound for at this time of day?" he inquired, pertinently.

The Bull pricked up his ears for the answer.

"I'm going for a Turkish bath," said Tom, in a clear and tranquil voice. "Beastly hot day."

His father gasped for speech. So did the Bull. The whole office had heard through the open door, and shivered and thrilled with emotion.

"I wouldn't stay and work too long," said Tom, in the same clear voice, to the Bull and Bear. "It's too hot to work. Better give the office a holiday."

With that he left them, stopped a moment at his desk to speak again to Merriam and give him his keys, then walked to the door.

"Tom!" called his father, weak with astonishment, but Tom did not look round.

"Norrie!" thundered the Bull in his deepest tones, starting after him.

But Tom walked on into the street, as if he heard nothing, and the Bull halted midway to the door, then turned back hastily and ignominiously to his sanctum, while a suppressed smile of joy and triumph lit the face of every clerk in the room. Tom passed by the windows, whistling lightly a popular song. He did not look in, but they all looked out at him—even the Bull and Bear—and as he was not visible again for many weary work days to the firm of Norrie, Trumbull & Co., they none of them forgot how boyish and nonchalant and gay he looked as he went along the street that hot afternoon of early spring—"the hottest April day in twenty-five years," as they all learned later from their evening papers.

CHAPTER II

THE COST OF MONEY

Upon leaving behind him the plate-glass windows of the great money-getting prison where he had spent in drudgery eight of the best years of his life, Tom Norrie's first concern was to call up a messenger-boy. This red-cheeked young rascal he despatched upon his errand with a great particularity of verbal instructions to supplement the note he had written. Then with his mind clear of care, he walked on to the main thoroughfare of the busy city, and leisurely followed that somewhat shabby street until he came to the Turkish and Russian baths. After some two hours he emerged, took the hansom which waited in response to his telephone call, and was driven to his club. Here, as he alighted from the cab, an ancient negro serving-man awaited him upon the pavement

"Well, Thaddeus, you got my message?" said Tom.

"Yessir, an' I done lef' you t'ings to de station, Mr. Tom," replied Thaddeus, his bald head of polished bronze bared to the warm breezes.

"You're sure you got everything I shall want?"

"Yessir; I berry partic'lar, Mr. Tom."

"And you kept your mouth shut?"

"You knows I don' do no talkin', Mr. Tom," said Thaddeus, with dignity;— "'specially to dem white ladies."

"Well, I'm glad you've a proper scorn for their color, Thaddeus," said Tom with a laugh, "though I wasn't aware that white ladies of the kitchen were any more given to conversation than black ones."

"If you don' want you' folks to know what I been about, Mr. Tom, I better be a-gettin' back, afore you' fader comes home to his supper."

"All right, Thaddeus, and here's a re-tainer for your discretion. Mind, whatever happens, you don't know anything about me!"

"I habn't seen or heard nuffin ob you since I done gib you you' breakfus dis mornin', Mr. Tom," declared Thaddeus, gravely shaking his head. The fringe of short white wool circling its bronze knob gave him a venerable aspect, and in the gravity and age of his countenance there was an expression of great benevolence—an expression possibly heightened by the shining yellow disk that lay in the copper-colored palm of his hand, and which he regarded covertly, as if in fear that it might not be all that its color and size seemed to indicate.

"That's right," said Tom, laughing, as he went up the club steps.

But Thaddeus did not yet go. "Mr. Tom," he said at the foot of the steps.

Tom turned. "Well?"

"I—I hope, Mr. Tom, you be careful ob youse'f."

"Why, yes, Thaddeus. Why should you think I wouldn't?" said Tom, amused.

"You—you's a fine young man, Mr. Tom, dough I say it as shouldn't, since I mos'ly brought you up myse'f. You don' want to begin now and do anyting you be sorry for. I notice dese last week or two dat sumfin's up—you ain't been youse'f, Mr. Tom."

"Oh, well, Thaddeus, I'm all right; you needn't worry," said Tom, kindly. He was touched at the old man's perception,

and laughed a little bitterly at the thought
that Thaddeus was, without doubt, the only
person who had observed the phenomena of
his emotions. He diverted his mind, however, from this rather melancholy reflection
by an intimate consultation with his favorite
waiter at the club as to what he should have
for his dinner.

" At seven o'clock sharp," he said, when
this matter was settled to his satisfaction,
and he left the café.

" Mr. Norrie's a very fine epicure," said
Ambrose, admiringly, to Philippe, as they
watched Tom down the steps.

" Yes," said Philippe, in the same tone,
to Ambrose.   " And they say he's the
member that puts all the five dollar gold
pieces in the Christmas-box.   Cooky ought
to look out for him."

" Cooky always does," returned Ambrose
as he went off to consult with that important
functionary.

Tom strolled up the wide street, in the
pleasant cool of the spring evening, until he
came to the railway station.   He bought a
ticket for Chicago, took a drawing-room
section on the night train, and arranged
about the luggage which Thaddeus had left

for him. Then he strolled back as he had come to the club, seeing no one, but lost in his contemplations as he had been throughout the whole day. The evening papers had no interest for him, and his friends were unobserved or barely nodded to. During the hour that he waited for his dinner, he sat by a window, in a luxurious low chair, gazing up into the mellow tones of the twilight sky ; and his silent but epicurean feast consumed, he returned to this chair, and sat there with his cigar throughout the evening, until it came time to go to the train, only bestirring himself when one cigar was finished and it became necessary to light another.

Tom Norrie had come that day to a momentous decision, and now, in the light of it, was reviewing his past life, considering life in general, what its meaning was, and what might make it worth while, and looking forward into his future—first the immediate future, then all that lay beyond, the years of his life yet to be lived.

He had been graduated from college at twenty-one, had spent that summer abroad, and had come home in September to plunge at once into " the business "—his father's business and his grandfather's business, the

business of his two uncles now retired, and
of a crop of cousins, both younger and
older than himself. The young men of the
family were drawn into it one by one as
they grew up; they had to leave pleasure
and self-improvement and all else behind, to
give their lives into the greedy maw of this
insatiable creature. Tom could think of it
in no other way but as a great devouring
beast, thirsting for human lives, sucking all
the sweetness and value out of them, taking
their youth, and strength and vigor, jeal-
ously exacting every whit—and giving what
in exchange?—money—miserable money,
bought with life-blood, paid for at usury,
and at a rate so high that nothing was left
with which to enjoy it. He had given so
much for his dollars that he despised them.
He had a thousand of them in his pocket
now, and he liked to throw them away, and
show himself how little they were worth—
how lightly he estimated what he had given
his manhood for.

Yes, his manhood—no less. He had
been a brave and happy boy, ready for
everything, afraid of nothing, full of interests, eager for the tussle with life. He had
had his tussle and been broken. At twenty-

nine he was nervous and dyspeptic—tired
out.   He could not sleep at night, things
worried him.   He was cautious, unwilling
to take risks, afraid of responsibility—yes,
as Janet had told him, in so many words,
he, Tom Norrie, was a coward.   He had
not seen it before she told him, nor would
he admit it to her; but now, to himself, he
admitted it all.   He was fussy, fidgety,
methodical, a very old granny in all his
habits and ways.

He had not been like that eight years ago
—it was the business that had done it, the
great relentless creature that had ground him
down to its uses and ruined his life.   He
thought of his college days, his gay life
with his comrades, his pleasures in the college sports, his love of boating and riding
and all else that one could do in the great
out-of-doors.   He was not an athlete, but he
was wiry, quick and dexterous, and had a
natural knack at handling himself and his
tool of the moment—the boat, the horse, the
racket, or cricket-bat.   Then, besides, he enjoyed his books—he was no scholar, but
neither was he a dunce, and he liked reading and had great plans of what he would
do in that way when college was over and

2

he had more time. He meant to travel, too, and see life, and know the world. His trip to Europe was in his mind but a fore-taste of future excursions in which he should explore one country after another, and get to know them intimately. He had the true traveller's instinct—an unflagging interest in things new and strange, a quick eye for pict-uresque differences of costume or manner, a delight in people in themselves, their indi-vidualities and eccentricities, a fine capacity for not being at all annoyed by things that at home would annoy him beyond measure, and a capacity still greater for never being bored. He had, too, in those days, an ad-venturous spirit—he liked a sense of risk in the undertaking, and the danger which brought all his blood to his heart never shook his nerve. Now—well, he was an old man before his time. The great relentless machine that had taken all this from him, crushed out the sap of the tree, and left a lifeless pulp, had paid him in worthless dol-lars—dollars that could not buy back a tithe of what he had lost.

He could never forget the first process of this change, the nightmare of his first year in the business. Two days after his arrival

home from Europe his father sent him down
to the office, telling him he had played long
enough, that now he was a man, and life
and work must begin for him.   He was at
once set to making out bills.   He reached
the office at eight o'clock, and made out
bills until half-past twelve.   He had then an
hour for his dinner, and came back and
made out bills again until six.   Then he
went home to supper, and was so fagged
with the unwonted confinement, nine hours
sitting at a desk, that he often went ignominiously to bed at half-past eight, or even
earlier.

" I shall soon get used to it," he thought,
hopefully.   " Then I can read in my even-
ings, and get on with the things I want to
do."

But it was not so easy, after all, to get
used to it.   When two or three months
were gone he was still as sleepy and jaded
after each day's drudgery as he had been at
the start.   His reading was uphill work,
and ended in yawns; then he would throw
down the dry volume of history, and take a
novel, and lose himself in this if he could.
If he were only able to forget everything
for a few hours he did not mind how much

sleep he lost, or how bad a headache he had
the next day.   He longed for work with interest in it, something he could think about,
put mind and energy into, and thus get from
it some enjoyment.   To make out bills all
day, every day, grew more and more terrible.   It became perfectly mechanical,
mere hand and eye work, that left him
nine blank hours in which to think.   It was
from his thoughts that he longed to get
away.   '' Is this to be the end of all my am-
bitions ? '' he asked himself.   '' Is all my life
to be like this ?   Must I work away at business, business, the sordid details of money-
getting, till I am an old man ?   Shall I grow
middle-aged and elderly doing this sort of
drudgery ?   Shall I still be doing it, like my
father, when I am sixty ?   Is that what life
means ?   Is that what I was born for, educated for ?   What is the good ?   What
makes it worth while ?   Why isn't it better
to die than be such a slave ? ''

His depression was terrible, and wholly
mastered him.   He was unable to force himself out of the dull silence of a fixed gloom.
His family thought he was sobering down
very quickly, but, busy with other things,
took little notice of his mood, and never un-

derstood the nightmare his life was to him—
the intense loathing he had for his work and
all related to it.   He was surrounded by the
commercial atmosphere.   " Business " was
so much a matter of course to every one
about him that he knew he could hope for
no sympathy, and so kept his blue devils to
himself.   Had not the family in all its
branches been made by business ?   Was not
all they had due to it ?   Did they not owe
to it not alone their life and breath, their
food and drink, but also their pleasure, their
position, everything ?   Was not the very
city in which they lived redolent of business, flavored as it were with the essential
extract of trade, commercial to its marrow ?
How he hated it—the narrow, ugly streets,
the flatness, the miles of brick houses, all
alike, all hideous, stretching into hideous
suburbs, where the brick boxes gave place to
architectural horrors in party-colored stone
—a city of Philistinism, of vulgarity, rich
and poor confounded in one garment of sordid mediocrity.

It seemed to him there could be no charm
or beauty in life amid such surroundings,
amid such a people.   He let himself hate the
people together with the town they lived

in.   His real friends were his old college
mates, scattered now about the world, and
none near him.   He made no new intimates
here.   His cousins, whom he saw daily, were
objects of a fascinated contemplation with
him.   What could they find in the dull routine of their lives to make it possible to live,
and apparently be happy?   They seemed to
think of nothing but dollars, bargains,
shrewd transactions of one sort or another.
They had no ideas, and not feeling the lack
of them never even read books to assimilate
those of others.   Their political anl relig-
ious opinions were to Tom bigoted anachro-
nisms, impossible even of peaceable discussion.   Their very wives, absorbed and worried
with housekeeping cares, and their children,
noisy, pert and forever underfoot, struck
this morbid youth as too vulgar and odious
to be endured.   It seemed to him almost a
crime to perpetuate so much that was unlove-
ly in large families of robust infants, who
would grow up to lead the same lives and
hand on the same dismal inheritance to suc-
cessive generations.

But this year of misery and morbidness
passed at last.   Tom received three hundred
dollars for his work; and had, in July, two

weeks of vacation. How he looked forward
to that vacation ! What hopes he had of ease
and pleasure, of freshening his mind, taking a new start, getting up his courage for
another year. He would rest a little first,
somewhere in grassy woods, far away from
the city, and all the city noise and turmoil.
Then, after a day or two lying on his back
under the trees and looking up through the
leaves at the clear sky, he would map out his
year before him, resolve to do certain work,
begin upon it then and there, and carry it
out in spite of all the sluggish weariness
that might beset him. He would not throw
his life away—become a mere machine for
doing figures—he would save a little of his
force for his own use, rescue his waning interests, and keep some life of his own beyond
the clutches of the greedy, jealous creature
that wanted all he had.

So he planned, looking forward to that
fortnight with an almost painful eagerness,
as to the only fountain in an arid desert—
his only chance for life. It came at last,
and then in a mere instant it was gone, and
somehow he had done nothing. He could
never understand it. Was the reaction too
great after so many weeks of work ? Was his

mind as flabby as he found his arm when he tried to play at tennis? It seemed to him afterwards that those two weeks had gone in a dream, mere dead lethargy, out of which he could not lift himself. He had dropped to the ground with a great sigh of relief, and when he was able at last to rouse himself the precious days were gone, the oasis was behind him, the cruel desert before him, and another long, dreary journey, for which he had no heart.

This disappointment left him more discouraged than ever, and even the great relief of a change in his work could not hearten him. He no longer made bills all day every day, yet the work he did do was as dead and meaningless. Nine hours of it left him physically too tired for anything but the lightest distraction in the evening, and hence the seeking of such distraction became with him a pursuit. If he could only forget what he had expected life to be he might be able to endure what it was!

Thus he became gradually a club man, a society man—anything to occupy his time and deaden his thoughts. The atmosphere of domesticity about his cousins, their too obvious flavor of bread and butter, the suburban sor-

didness of their matrimonial joys, drove him
into revolt.   By way of uttering his protest
against their provincial manners, he attired
himself nightly in evening costume and assumed so far as he might the habits of a
more cosmopolitan world. This immediately
brought upon him in the family circle the
accusation of being fast ; it was even darkly
hinted that he drank wine and was on his
way to become a cynical man of the world.
The futility of the charge was proved by the
young man's delight in it and his eagerness
to make the fact patent to all his relatives.
He made formal evening calls from time to
time at their houses, where he refused the
discomfort incident to being made "one of
the family," preferred the quiet of the stiff
little parlors to the hubbub of the general
sitting-rooms, ignored the children if they
were allowed to appear, and became silent
and changed the subject if they or the servants or family gossip were introduced into
the conversation, which he insisted on keeping upon high general planes of literature,
music, and art.   He admitted on these occasions grave doubts in regard both to marriage and religion, and delivered himself of
sundry cheap cynicisms about women, after

what he thought the true manner of a real man of the world. In short, for the time being he forgot his sense of humor in this worldly pose, while he succeeded only in making himself extremely disagreeable. Perhaps, after all, the most obnoxious prig is the modern sort, who rejects instead of upholding the faith of his fathers and represents himself as shocked by the old ideas instead of by the new. For there may easily be "a priggishness in avoiding priggishness; when men think to do best if they go furthest from the priggishness formerly received."

But at least Tom's mind was occupied by those doubtful pleasantries, nor was it long before he began to see the ludicrous side of taking himself so seriously. For as time went on the first morbidness of his misery inevitably passed away, and with the return of a more healthy tone of mind his really excellent sense of humor reasserted itself. Humor is the basis of common sense, and, indeed, of most of the virtues which make people easy to live with, and their own lives possible to themselves. Tom began to see that it was necessary to occupy himself fully in all his leisure moments, rationally or irrationally, as the case might be. The main thing was to be occupied, and this, at last, he succeeded in accomplishing without the sense of working for it. He got to know quantities of people—he had engagements with them, which he kept religiously—he gave importance to all sorts of more or less trifling pursuits—he became an amateur connoisseur in etchings, old china and bric-a-brac—he grew more and more interested in the decoration of his apartments, more and more fastidious about what he had to eat, and more and more concerned over the details of his attire.

Thus the days passed into months, and the months into years, and Tom Norrie was not an unhappy man, because no one who is busy all the time can be unhappy. Some leisure is necessary if one is to enjoy one's melancholy, and Tom left himself never a moment's leisure in his days, while each one " brought its petty dust his soon-choked soul to fill," and at times he almost forgot that he had anything he wanted to forget.

Yet what a trivial unmeaning life it was, if he ever did allow himself to stop for a moment and think! And it was impossible not to drop the curb sometimes, and give his thoughts free rein. Then all the nausea

of that first year came back on him in full
force, and he asked himself again if this
was life. Should he grow old and gray in
this dull routine, this merely hand-to-mouth
existence, with no real purpose except to
make money enough to pay the bills con-
tracted in the process of making the money?
It was like the man who couldn't get along
without his horse, because he had to drive
five miles every fortnight to get oats to feed
him on. His own life seemed to him just as
illogical, just as ridiculous as that.

There was some consolation in the facts
that he was very successful in the work he
hated so, and that he had all the money he
wanted, and more. He had stuck so doggedly
at his tasks that he had mastered the detail
of the business with a swiftness that as-
tonished his seniors. At twenty-five, though
he had never received from either his father
or Mr. Trumbull a word of encouragement
or praise, he suddenly found himself a partner, with a great income of his own. He
hated the money, yet he liked it, and he
spent it lavishly to help him forget that it
was after all only a bribe, the purchase-
money of his soul. He wondered vaguely
now and then that he made no move, that he

stayed on there so tamely, and took the bribe
each year; but the question was answered
in the occupation of the next moment, and
then there was something else to do after that,
and so his life went on, one day at a time,
giving him little chance to think of such
troublesome things as the past and the future.

And then, finally, he met Janet Trumbull,
and everything took on a new color from
its association with her. Certainly he could
never have asked her to marry him if he
had not had plenty of money, and the money
came from the despised business. He began
to look back on those years of unhappiness
as his period of service for his Rachel—bitter
service, but what an adorable and fascinating Rachel! He must settle down like
other men, and settling down cost money,
and money meant work, but no work was
too much for such a prize.

Miss Janet, however, proved a very modern Rachel, with little inclination to "settle
down," and he began vaguely to fear that
his years of service were only begun instead
of ended. And now, at last, it was all over
—she had jilted him, and he had nothing to
console him but the business. He rejected
this consolation immediately, vindictively,

finally, and cast from his feet with scorn the
hated dust of the office of Norrie, Trumbull
& Co.   He was a free man for the first time
in eight years—but a free man now forever.

He tried to feel bitter towards Janet for
the pain and humiliation she had caused
him.   Yet but for her he would still have
been a slave, a prisoner in chains, and how
could he feel anything but gratitude towards
the one who had brought about his freedom ?
Freedom meant, besides, a chance to prove
himself not a coward.   Perhaps he was a
coward, through and through—he felt un-
easily uncertain of himself.   But at least he
would give himself a chance, and if there
were left any of the old courage or lightness
of heart, he would exploit it for all it was
worth.   Janet should see, he said impulsively
to himself, with a resolute brow—and then
he laughed at his folly, for what difference did
he make to Janet now, or she to him ?   He
no longer cared for her—and no woman was
worth a man's freedom, anyway.   He really only cared to prove himself not a coward
for his own satisfaction.   Janet was a creature
of the past—he should probably never see her
again—and she would be sure to marry some
rich old molly-coddle, afraid of his shadow.

CHAPTER III

LESSONS IN LOVE-MAKING

Tom had seen Janet Trumbull many times when she was a schoolgirl in short dresses. He considered her a pretty little hoyden then, and forgot all about her. She, meanwhile, continued her education, went to college, and grew up with great rapidity.

The Norries and the Trumbulls, in spite of the business connection, were not intimate with each other socially. The Norries lived north of a certain street—the unfashionable side—and the Trumbulls south of it; the Norries were Friends, the Trumbulls Church people; the Norries dined at midday, the Trumbulls at night; and these differences were far too vital to be offset by any ordinary respect and affection incident to business association. Mr. Norrie, however, dined once a year at the Trumbulls', and Mr. and Mrs. Trumbull took supper as often at the Norries'; and, when Tom be-

came a member of the firm Mr. Trumbull
deemed it appropriate to ask the young man
also to the house once or twice in the season.
Tom always accepted in duty bound, knowing that there would be a good dinner, good
wine, and a few good jokes from the Bull,
but expecting otherwise a rather oppressive
entertainment.

But at one of these periodical feasts Miss
Janet made her appearance, and Tom did
not find the entertainment oppressive that
evening. He called very soon afterwards,
and very soon again after that, and shortly
established himself on a familiar footing in
the family, at which the young lady's gruff
papa sniffed humorously, but without dis-
pleasure.

Miss Janet was a personable young woman, tall, slender and dark, whom the higher
education had taught at least to hold her
head very high. She had a quick sense of
humor and a nice turn for sarcasm, and
proved a very difficult young person to pay
court to, on account of a pronounced tendency to laugh at all suggestions of sentiment. She was strictly a modern girl, as
became her college training, and had very
modern notions of men and marriage; she

was by no means sure that she cared to have
much to do with them. But training cannot do away with nature, and Janet's nature
was that perennially fascinating and always
womanly one that can't help liking men and
liking to be liked by them. She was the
kind of girl who is so attractive that she is
accused, early and often, of being a flirt—
and perhaps Janet did flirt a little now and
then, though it was entirely against her
principles to do so. At all events she led
her father's partner, Mr. Thomas Norrie,
Jr., a very lively dance through the first
winter of their acquaintance, and made that
ardent young man despair of ever bringing so top-lofty a head under the yoke of
matrimony. But he wooed in earnest and
he wooed well. He realized the importance of the method in that time-honored
pursuit and tried to be bold, always bold,
but not overbold; to adjust with tactful
nicety the degree of his presumption, and
temper it well with the most attentive service.

It is one of the lovable weaknesses of a
nature such as Miss Janet's that it is sure to
carry its liking to be liked a thought too
far some day—to care too much to be ad-

3

mired by one man in especial, and to end by
finding itself in love with him, by dint of
thinking so much about him.   Tom Norrie
was six years her senior, and in her eyes he
was a fastidious man of the world, whose
admiration would be, in a way, a stamp of
perfection.   She set about winning it with
all her maidenly art, aided by all the lore
and the accomplishments of a college-bred
girl.   And however obvious the attainment
of the end was to all about her, she was
never herself quite certain that Tom Norrie
didn't disapprove of her until he suddenly
proposed marriage to her in the back garden
one agreeable spring evening in the light of
the silver moon.

They had had their coffee there after dinner, and now her mother was gone in, and
she was lying back in the steamer-chair, her
hand dropped on the rug at her side, looking up at the moon through the twisted and
half-clad branches of a great buttonwood.
Mr. Norrie had drawn his stool close to her
side after her mother's departure, and now,
as he declared himself, in a low and soft
voice, with broken statements of his affection very different from the eloquent periods
in which he had always previously said it

over to himself, he took possession of her drooping hand. The young lady lay quite still, looking at him, saying nothing, and making no effort to recover that piece of her property. Tom took heart from this apparent concession—indeed, he felt very sure that she liked him or he should not have committed himself so far—and bent forward with a swift motion as if to draw her to him.

" Janet, do you love me ? " he murmured.

" No," said Janet, sitting up straight, avoiding the threatened embrace, and possessing herself of her own hand. " That is— I hope not," she added in a moment, as if with a conscientious desire not to tell an untruth.

Tom, who had dropped from heaven the instant before, reascended half-way upon this, and then waited in a state of suspense, or perhaps better, suspension, for further developments. "Ah, but if you're not sure ! " he murmured. " Then I sha'n't give you up —I shall make you care for me."

" I forbid you to do any such thing," said Janet, quickly. " I don't want to care for you—I should much rather not—and— and—I'm very glad I'm going away next week."

This struck Tom as a trifle inconclusive. He arose and took a stroll about the grass, his hands in his pockets and his head bent forward in profound thought about the peculiar ways of women. Should he press his point, or give her her own way? Which would be the better, the surer method? He must not drive her into rebellion, and neither must she feel any weakness or hesitation in his attitude towards her. It was difficult to control himself now. He had so nearly had her in his arms a moment since, and she was so lovely, so wild, so defiantly dear! He took another turn or two about, before he went back and sat down on his stool, this time drawing it off to a more discreet distance, with half the length of the rug between it and the steamer-chair.

"Do you mind if I smoke?" he asked in a polite and conversational tone.

Janet gasped, but managed to utter a somewhat inarticulate consent to this unexpected request.

"I have to go soon," went on Tom, "but I'll smoke this one cigar first, and perhaps you'll tell me a little about your plans. I had no idea you were to begin your summer outing so early."

The young lady's account of her plans was very confused, and Tom's heart beat with inward delight at her agitation. He managed to gather that an unencumbered aunt in New York, who was very fond of her niece and very fond of travelling, had invited her to go on an out-of-the-way sort of trip to the Sandwich Islands, to Samoa and Japan, that the invitation had but just come, and that the answer was not yet sent, but that she had made up her mind to go, and would probably leave in eight days at the outside.

" It sounds like the most charming trip imaginable," said Tom. " I would certainly let nothing interfere with it if I were you. You are very much to be envied to have such a chance. I hope it will be perfect in every way, and that you'll have lots of fun. You are going so soon that I don't believe I shall see you again, so I'll wish you bon voyage now. Don't come in — it is too lovely out here. I can find your mother by myself."

Janet was not able to utter a word in reply to all this easy volubility, and she sat in blank silence after Tom left her. What had she done? Did he really care at all? How could he talk and act so if he did? It had taken so little to dampen his ardor ! If she

had had any idea—Her mind reverted to
the thrill that went through her when he
began speaking in that soft, ardent voice,
and took her hand.   How close and warm
his clasp was !   She had been lulled into a
sort of dream, unable to resist.   It was only
when he moved nearer to her and she felt the
response to him through her whole being that
she had stirred herself to resistance.   Well,
if it needed so little as that to scare him off
he might go—she would not call him back.
If she loved a girl she would woo more man-
fully, more masterfully—she would not give
in at the first rebuff.   Not that she wanted a
master, or would even acknowledge one ; but
if a man wasn't strong and manly he wasn't
worth loving and marrying.   The way to
make marriage the equal affair it should be
was for the woman to be just as strong and
just as manly—not for the man to be less
so.   A sudden idea struck her.   Well, why
shouldn't she ?   It would be a capital object-
lesson for him.

> 'Tis not so much the gallant who woos
> As the gallant's way of wooing !

She strolled up and down on the grass as
Tom had done, and in much the same cir-

cuit, but with her hands posed on her hips instead of in pockets, her head high in the air instead of bent forward, while she punctuated her thoughts with smiles and laughs, and tossings of her head—as if to get it still higher—and finally a sudden clapping of her hands.

" That's exactly it ! " she cried aloud. " I'll give him four days. And then if he hasn't come back I'll do it—I will ! It will be too much fun ! "

Thus Tom, growing daily more dubious of the success of his bold methods, and sitting at his desk in the office with a longer face and longer, until there was no further possibility of elongation without fracture, received on the fifth day of waiting a strange and enigmatical note, which caused his heart to thrill with eager conjecture. The note was addressed to him, in Miss Trumbull's vigorous handwriting, but it began " Sweet Chloe," and ended, " Your never-to-be-daunted Strephon." Though Mr. Norrie was entirely unacquainted with either the gentleman or the lady, and had no right if he were to read their private correspondence, he perused this brief epistle with shameless eagerness.

"I am not the craven I seem," wrote Strephon. "A laggard in love is no lover, a coward in love is no man. I am both man and lover, and to prove this to you, with your gracious permission, fair lady, I will be beneath the plane-tree in the garden, where last I saw you, at nine to-night. I could, if needful—not being a coward, as I remarked before—scale the area fence from the back alley and risk the cruel hurts of the broken bottles glued on the top thereof, but unless you specially require this proof of the profundity of my passion, I should prefer that you would leave the gate unlocked. But through flood or fire, broken glass or barbed wire, I shall pass all barriers that lie betwixt us, and cast myself at your feet at the hour and place stated above, provided, of course, your feet are there to cast myself at. You furnish the feet and I'll do the rest, in other words. Is it a bargain?—if you will pardon the language of commerce applied to the affairs of love. And don't forget that I'm not a coward."

Tom Norrie, in evening dress, sneaking into a narrow back alley by moonlight in the deepest shadow he could find, dodging ash-barrels and scaring wandering cats, felt curiously unlike the nineteenth century and the prosaic workaday world in which he lived. He was not sure at first from the back which was the Trumbull mansion, and was aware that in the eyes of the police his hesitating actions would be highly suspicious. But the eyes of the police, as is usual on occasions of suspicion, were not there to see, and the mottled trunk of the great buttonwood distinguished it clearly in the moonlight from the tulip-trees and maples in the gardens round-about, and then in another moment his hand was on the latch of the gate, which yielded at once and swung open easily before him.

Tom almost laughed at the way his heart beat as he stepped within the charmed precinct. No one was visible. The rug, the bench, the steamer-chair, the wicker table, the stool, were all there, in exactly the positions they had occupied when he bade Janet farewell so coolly, five nights earlier. The dappled shadows cast by the sparse foliage of the buttonwood-tree lay over all, and the silence, even there in the heart of the city, seemed for the moment absolute. Tom took the precaution to lock the gate behind him, then waited for Chloe—or was he waiting

for Strephon ?   He really was not quite certain, the note having left him a little topsy-
turvy as to his own identity.   He leaned
against the rough trunk of Strephon's plane-
tree, which was certainly more poetical and
quite as correct as the buttonwood, and regarded the house, and the line of tall firs
which separated it from the garden, and cut
off all view of its lower story.   A church
clock not far away rang out nine on the
evening air, and promptly at the last stroke,
as seemed eminently consistent with the
solemn mystery of the occasion, a dark figure emerged from behind these firs and
paced slowly along the greensward towards
the spot where Mr. Norrie stood.   This mysterious shape paused at the distance of some
twenty feet, and Tom observed that it was
clad in a student's cap and gown.

" I would suggest," it said, in deep and
solemn tones, " that Miss Chloe remove her
top hat—top hats being not only inappropriate to her sex and condition, but a trifle
of an anachronism, to boot."

Tom instantly did as he was bid.

" Sit down," then commanded the shape.
" No—not there—in the low chair.   Now
lean back—so—and look up at the moon—

that's it. And in case you should feel chilly in your evening frock, here's a wrap to drape about your shoulders. Dear, no!—don't bundle it that way—you look as if you'd an awful cold in your head—arrange it with more coquetry and grace. Well, but you are clumsy!''

"I think if Strephon had any gallantry he might arrange it for me, instead of calling me names," grumbled Chloe.

"I didn't know you would permit such familiar attentions from your gen'lemen-friends," replied Strephon, with a laugh, but making no effort to relieve Chloe's embarrassment with the fleecy wrap. He drew up the stool and placed it exactly where Tom had sat when he made his momentous declaration. "Now we're ready to begin," he declared, sitting down and regarding Chloe.

Tom looked at the girl's mischievous face, half darkened by the shadow of her mortarboard, and wondered what she was up to.

"She shall work it her own way," he said to himself. "I'll not interfere in the very least."

Strephon leaned forward toward Chloe on the steamer-chair and composed his features to as impressive and serious an expression as possible. " Chloe," he said, in a low and thrilling voice, " we have known each other well hardly more than half a year. I could tell you the very moment of our meeting, and how many hours we have spent in each other's society up to date, but until I am sure of the nature of your sentiments towards me I refrain from wearying you with arithmetical details that might remind you of my methodical commercial habits. Nor do I say that I fell in love with you at first sight, for that would not be true, and I wish to be as exact in the affairs of love as in those of trade, exactitude being an admirable business habit. Besides, I wish especially to make the point that I have not loved you long in secret, and put off telling you until I felt sure you reciprocated, for fear of having my pride hurt by refusal. On the contrary, I never realized the state of my affections until I spoke to you so abruptly the other evening, and then the only reason why I stopped talking about it and went off at your first ' No ' was because I remembered a very important engagement I had at my club, which I had forgotten up to that identical minute. Duty called me and I had

to go, but I left my heart at your feet—
where it has remained ever since for all I
know, and I hope you haven't been playing
football with it."

Strephon here looked about suspiciously
for the missing organ referred to, but not
seeing it, resumed his remarks. "Of course
I am aware that my behavior strongly resembled cowardice—it certainly looked as if
I feared the word ' No ' as a raw recruit
would a cannon-ball, and fled at the first
volley in order to be out of sight and sound
of the second. But that was not so, Chloe ;
I don't like to hear you say ' No,' I admit,
but I am ready to hear it forty times if there
is the slightest chance of a ' Yes ' at the
forty-first. And to prove this I am here to-
night, to stand to my colors and be shot at
my post if need be. At least I shall die a
soldier, on the field of battle, fighting for
what is dearest to me, and what better fate
can there be than that ? Besides, I am well
aware "—here Strephon's voice became very
significant in its tone—" that women care
for nothing in men so much as for courage ;
so, even if I were quaking and shivering inside, which I'm not, I should still force myself to take this bold stand, knowing that if

there were any chance for me whatever this would be the way to win it."

Strephon stopped a moment impressively, looking at Chloe with all his eyes, as the saying goes. " Chloe," he declared, " I love you. I ask you again—do you love me?"

Chloe, who had been lying in her chair quite passively, with her hands in her lap, seemed suddenly at this point to remember something, and instead of answering Strephon's question, quickly lifted one arm, and let her hand drop over the side of the chair to the rug below.

Strephon grinned appreciatively at this manœuvre, but hesitated a moment, as if the duty before him were very repugnant. "I must not falter now," he murmured to himself, but quite audibly; and then, in a somewhat gingerly manner, picked up Chloe's hand and looked at it as if he did not know what to do with it. "I can stand cannonballs," he said, in a stage aside, "but hand to hand encounters are more than I bargained for." However, he took the hand in his, with a very creditable pressure, and resumed his discourse. "You do not answer me, Chloe. Again I ask, do you love me—can you love me?"

Chloe now pulled her hand away (it was
an heroic effort on the part of Mr. Norrie)
and sat upright. "No, I don't," she said,
somewhat viciously. "Maybe I could if I
would, but I wouldn't if I could."

Strephon smiled at the familiar vehemence of these remarks. "All right," he
said, cheerfully, "but I don't give up the
ship, all the same. I'll side track a little
bit, for variety, and then we'll come back
to the main line again." Whereupon he
launched into a vigorous enumeration of
Chloe's charms, and of the reasons why he
loved her. "Of course," he wound up,
"I am aware that what a woman likes best
in a man next to courage is compliments,
but that is not the reason I am telling you
all these things. I am telling them to you
because they are true—not to curry favor.
They may not interest you in the least, but
they are facts all the same. Now, Chloe,
I ask you once more—do you love me?"

Chloe had placed her hand at this juncture
very obviously on her knee, within a foot of
Strephon's, but that young man apparently
felt no temptation to touch it. Chloe sniffed
contemptuously, and replied again, "No, I
don't—that is—I hope not. When I do

fall in love I hope it may be with a man—
who will make use of his opportunities."

Strephon looked a little dubious at this.
"Thrice refused," he said, after a moment.
"Well, I think that will do for to-night's
cannonading. But I give you fair warning,
Chloe, that I intend to fight it out on this
line if it takes all summer. I shall adopt all
known methods of warfare, and shall never
give up the siege—unless—unless the city
surrenders to another commander. Then,
and then only, shall I fold my tents and
move away. But for the present—farewell."

Strephon started to rise, but Chloe threw
herself forward on her knees at his side, and
forcibly prevented his departure—yet with
a very delicate force, as befitted her sex.

"No—no, Janet, not so fast," said Tom.
"You have given me a lesson—now I must
return the favor. Do you really think any
Chloe would care for so cold and unimpas-
sioned a Strephon, who held her hand as if
it were a piece of wood, and dropped it at
the first excuse? No, my dear girl—you've
a great deal yet to learn about love-making,
and I should like nothing so much as to be
your teacher. I'd not charge you a cent for
tuition, either—I'd do it for love."

"It's a branch I'm not at all anxious to take up—yet," said Janet. "And, really, Mr. Norrie, I can't see what right you have to hold my hands. You don't do it in the least as if they were pieces of wood!"

"It's an object-lesson," declared Tom, boldly. "I'm showing you how it ought to be done. You evidently had not the least idea —and—and—well, knowledge is power." He drew her hands against his heart with a sudden impassioned gesture. "And you call me a coward," he murmured, "and have no idea of the courage of a man who puts himself constantly in the way of the strongest temptation, and yet resists it. The brave man fights his battles within himself, and the undiscerning, hearing no blare of trumpets nor clash of warfare, see only what they call weakness—cowardice! My heart is burning with love of you—I would give all I possess to take you in my arms—press you to my heart—yet I sit here calmly—— "

"Kneel," prompted Janet, mischievously.

"Kneel here calmly, and discourse to you jokingly of this thing and that, as if you were no more to me than your plane-tree yonder—as if we were both blocks of wood, instead of throbbing flesh and blood."

4

"Don't call me names," said Janet, "I don't throb."

Tom looked at her fixedly. "I'll venture the contrary," he said, in the low, ardent tone that had thrilled her so the other night. "You do care for me in spite of yourself—your heart is responsive to me—it does throb with strange and new emotions, now, as I tell you of my love—and if I draw it to mine and hold you there—close—never to let you leave me again— you will not repulse me—you cannot—love is stronger than you, and you must yield to its power."

Some moments later Janet broke the silence by observing, in a lightly conversational tone, "I think I'll change my mind and take up Love after all. I learned most other things at college—so I've really plenty of time, and this seems an excellent opportunity. So cheap, too—I don't know where I could have found such an excellent professor at such advantageous rates. It will interfere a little with my summer plans, to be sure—but I shall be improving my mind all the time, at least. However, I must consult mamma and papa about it, and see if they approve——"

"Oh, not yet," begged Tom, "it's so pleasant out here!"

" Is it ? " asked Janet, with an incredulous little laugh.

" Besides," went on Mr. Norrie, in the same persuasive accents, " I should like to suggest—of course if you're to study with me I'm anxious to have my pupil as proficient as possible, and the more time you spend on it the quicker you learn, you know—er—er —why shouldn't we get married ? "

" Married ! "   The young lady was standing upright and indignant six feet away, and Tom had a sensation of being scattered to the four winds as he rose in confusion from his kneeling posture.

" I don't know why that should surprise you so," he said, ruefully.   " The very first lesson in love, before you've learned to conjugate it even, is that it must end in marriage, that marriage is its logical outcome——"

" Ah ! But to commit yourself to it forever before you've learned the first syllable, before you know whether you like it or not ? The idea ! Besides,"—flippantly—" even if I enjoyed the study I might prefer to change my professor ! No, Mr. Norrie ; it is one of the advantages of college training for women that it teaches them not to be precipitate in their choice of life—not to marry too young. If you care to go on with this instruction I am ready also, but on the imperative condition that marriage is not again mentioned by you for a year ! "

" Oh, well," said Tom, fatuously, "of course I'll accept any conditions, but I shall confide in your generosity, and trust that you won't be too hard on me."

Janet laughed. " I think you've a good deal to learn yourself, Mr. Professor," she remarked. " However, I'll undertake your tuition while you are busy with mine ; and so, even if you are sadder, you will at least be wiser ! "

CHAPTER IV

A QUESTION OF COURAGE

Almost a year of this mutual tuition had passed, and Tom, as Janet had predicted, was indeed sadder as well as wiser. The first six months had been woven nearly all of joy, for even when Janet was away in the summer there were her delightful letters during the week, and the still more delightful Sundays, passed together in forest walks in the mountains or by the sands of the sounding sea. She proved a coy and wayward lover, difficult to tame and shy of caresses, but Tom found great charm in this wildness, and tried hard not to disturb her with his own more impassioned notions of love-making.

But as the autumn wore on into the winter, and she still would hear no word of marriage, and seemed to grow more wilful rather than less so, the young man became impatient, and sometimes let her see it; or, again, de-

manded tenderness of her in her least
tender moods, and was hurt and unhappy
when she laughed in his face. At times he
felt as if he really knew her less than before he first spoke to her of his love. There
was a coldness, almost resentment, in the
way she looked at him, as if she could not
forgive him for having forced his way into
her private life. They seemed terribly remote and unknown to each other then, two
wholly separate beings, whose efforts to
enter into each other's hearts had only
shown them, with a bitter reality, that such
union was impossible—that men and women,
after all, must live in the world as they enter
it, and leave it, alone.

Janet had her softened moments, when she
too regretted this state of things, but their
attempts to talk it out and start fresh in
happier relations only ended in disagree-
ments, and an intensified misunderstanding.
Then Janet would be perverse, mischievous
and flippant, and Tom would get out of pa-
tience with her, and be exacting, or, still
more foolishly, denunciatory. Whereupon
Miss Janet would openly deride him, with
wicked sauciness, becoming even spiteful as
he persisted in his gloomy disapproval. Or

when he varied the program by being hurt and grieved, she would seem driven to complete exasperation by his unhappy expression, and then would treat him with contemptuous cruelty.   These fits were always followed by penitence, and a great kindness towards the victim, but as they increased in number and severity and the spasms of kindness grew briefer in proportion, Tom at last lost heart altogether, and went about in an utterly dejected way that made him anything but a pleasant companion to Janet or any one else.

And at last, only yesterday evening, they had had their final explanation, and now all was over between them forever. " Forever " —it is such a delightfully high-sounding word—even the most unhappy of discarded lovers derives a certain satisfaction from rolling it off the tip of his tongue, and gloats a little over the permanence of misery that it implies.

" Come, Tom, do be cheerful, and try to smile at least once in ten minutes," Miss Janet had said when her lover and his long face had graced the Trumbull drawing-room with a fixed melancholy for half an hour.

" I have nothing to smile about."

" " Very well, then, go away, and don't come back until you have something to smile about."

" I think perhaps that would be best myself."

" I am sure of it."

" Are you in earnest, Janet ? "

" Are not you ? "

" Yes. If my sadness exasperates you I'd better go away, since only your love can make me smile, and that you do not give me."

" Humph," with a shrug of the shoulders, " I certainly can't lavish affection upon you as long as you are so frightfully solemn, so I'm afraid it's a deadlock."

" Janet, we must be frank with each other ; I demand frankness."

" Tom," mimicking, " we have been frank with each other, and it always made us ' mad.' "

" Don't mock, Janet. I can't stand this sort of thing any longer. It's ruining my health."

The young lady regarded him scornfully. " You do look ill," she said, in a jeering tone, " positively emaciated. I don't believe you weigh more than ten pounds above what you did a year ago.''

'' A man needn't lose flesh to be ill,'' said Tom, gloomily.

'' Come, Tom ; don't be a baby. That's my great quarrel with you——''

'' What do you mean ? ''

'' You pity yourself too much. Your own sympathy with your woes is so excessive that it makes other people hard on you, just by reaction.''

'' I've noticed your hardness——''

''Of course ; I can't help it. I get so provoked with you for taking yourself so seriously, and regarding yourself as such an injured being. It—well, really, it doesn't seem to me manly.''

'' Does your conduct seem to you woman-ly ? ''

'' It doesn't seem to me anything ; I don't think about it. If I did I think yours would seem to me a sufficient excuse for all that was bad in it.''

'' So that I am all to blame ? ''

'' I shouldn't use that expression. I don't suppose you can help it.''

'' Help what ? ''

'' Being a—a——''

" Well ? "

" Oh, a baby—a coward—anything you choose to call it."

A long pause followed, during which Janet twitched a flower to pieces, and Tom sat in horrified silence regarding her.

" Do you really consider me a coward, Janet ? " he asked at last.

" That's what I said, didn't I ? "

" Why did you never tell me so before ? "

" I have — a hundred times — but you couldn't see it."

" You never used the word——"

" I implied it in a hundred ways—I supposed you knew what I meant."

" How implied it ? "

" Oh, I can't remember now—I've tried so many different methods ! Why, when you proposed to me, and went off et the first ' No '—all my mummery about Strephon and Chloe was meant to show that—that no such faint-heart could win a woman's love."

" It seems to me my method worked very well—with one woman," said Tom, coldly —" even if you did think me a faint-heart. It took but five days to bring you round."

" Method—five days ! " cried Janet, with flashing eyes. " Do you mean to say you planned that?—that you expected me to 'come round' as you call it? That was more cowardly even than I thought!"

"Don't be absurd, Janet. How can one say what one plans or doesn't plan at such a time of emotion? And besides, in love and war——"

"I think we've tried love long enough," said Janet, icily. "Suppose we try war now."

"It seems to me we've tried nothing else for the last few months. Calling it love didn't alter its real nature."

"Suppose, then, we try—nothing—for a change."

"Janet, say plainly what you mean. Do you wish to break our engagement?" Tom was very pale as he asked this question, and Janet shrank a little from the fixed severity of his expression, and seemed to find it impossible to make the answer she wished to make. "Answer me, Janet," demanded the young man. "This state of uncertainty has lasted long enough. I must know exactly what you wish."

"I wish to be free," she answered him in a low tone. Then, having at last said it, she was able to go on without restraint. "I can't stand being tied to you—it makes me almost hate you. I don't know why, for I know I loved you—once. Perhaps I love you still, but I never can find out so long as I am bound to you—so long as I must marry you whether I will or not. I can't bear the thought of marriage. I don't feel towards you as a woman should towards the man she is going to marry. I am impatient with you —critical of you—unjust to you, I am afraid."

" It is pleasant of you to admit the possibility of that," said Tom, bitterly.

" Why do you take that tone ? Do you suppose I want to treat you unkindly and make you miserable? Do you think I enjoy it and am very happy myself? Oh, Tom, you complain of my hardness, my lack of sympathy for you, and yet you yourself have never once taken the trouble to put yourself in my place and imagine how I must feel. It exasperates me — your concern about your own feelings, with never a thought of mine. You pity yourself so much—it is babyish. I want to think of you as manly and strong, but I can't. You seem to show your worst and weakest side to me ; I can't lean on you, I can't respect you. When-

ever I want your help you fail me. You
pretend to love me so much, but all you seem
to want of my love is what I can give you—
sympathy for you, admiration for you, interest in your affairs, your thoughts, your life—
and you forget entirely that I, too, am a human being, even if I'm not a man ; that I
have a life and thoughts and affairs, that I
want sympathy and interest and—and admiration———"

Tom was looking at her with a strange
calmness—the calmness of suppressed feeling.
" Do you really think I don't love you,
Janet—that my love is a mere selfish pretence ? " he asked, after some moments had
passed.

" Oh, you think you love me, Tom, of
course, but it doesn't seem to me real love.
Bah !—I hate the very name of love—it cov-
ers so much false sentiment, so many impossible ideals, such exacting selfishness ! It
means so much weariness and monotony and
boredom. Just think, Tom, of this year that
we have been engaged—what an awful waste
of time ! I don't believe you've read a book,
and I know I've not read many. Every
evening that we haven't been out together
you've spent here with me, and what have

we done ?   Just made love—nothing else ;
talked personalities and sentiment by the
hour, until I die of weariness to think of it.
So many times we should both of us rather
have read—or done anything, in fact, to
employ our minds rationally.   But, no, we
were engaged.   The thought that we could
possibly tire of each other's conversation was
not to be entertained for a moment !   It is
the convention of the situation that you must
make love ; it may bore you, but you must
do it ; it is the proper thing.   Ugh !   How
any rational woman can go through ' being
engaged,' and endure the thought of marriage—the perpetuation of it forever, I can't
see.   The whole situation is so false—you
have to pretend all the time.   I—I like to
be honest—to say and do what I like, express my feelings, even if they aren't the
thing that's expected of me.''

   '' That's your idea, I suppose, of purely un-
selfish love ? '' suggested Tom, sardonically.

   '' It's my idea of an equal and beautiful
relation, in which perfect honesty is possible.
Why shouldn't I have the right to say so if
love-making bores me ?—if I'm tired of bill-
ing and cooing and would rather read a book ?
If I don't feel in an affectionate mood and

would rather not be kissed? Oh, Tom, I want no more of what you call love—this winter has been a nightmare to me! You've exacted affection of me when it nauseated me; talked personalities until I was bored to death, growing silent and unexpressive once your favorite subjects were abandoned; regarding love as a thing purely of the senses, with no food for the mind—and my mind has been so unsatisfied! Then if I gave the slightest expression to any of this feeling, you were so sensitive, and your sensitiveness was sufficient excuse in your mind for any degree of limpness and loppiness and general prostration that you chose to indulge in. I had to be comforting you and coddling you all the time, and binding up your wounds, and treating you like a baby, and saying things I didn't mean, just to get you cheerful again. I've always been honest, and I like to be honest, but this year of our engagement I've told more white lies, acted more untruths than I ever dreamed would be possible for me, and all just to gloss over the injuries done to your sensitive disposition! Sensitiveness is only another name for selfishness, I think —and such a weak, mushy sort of selfishness! I know I'm perfectly hateful, but if being

engaged to you makes me so I'd certainly
better stop being engaged. And I know
there's another side—your side—and I can
see it much more vividly than you think,
and feel far more miserable than I could
make you believe to cause you such suffering
as this. But I can't help it ; there's no use
in keeping up this sort of a farce, and pre-
tending to feel what I don't feel.''

" I can tell you what the whole trouble is,''
said Tom. "You have never loved me—
you have loved an ideal manufactured in
your own brain, and because I prove, naturally, very unlike this paragon, you think me
one delusion and all love another. But
there is one thing I cannot understand, and
that is why my inability to come up to the
standard of your pattern man should necessi-
tate your calling me a coward.''

" Can you prove that you aren't ? ''

" The burden of proof is on you.''

" Well, I suppose really it is more a suspicion—a fear with me—than anything else.
I've always adored strength and courage in
men and women alike, and the fear that you
mightn't have them was torture to me. The
least suspicion of weakness in you made me
harsh and hard towards you, and the least

lack of resolution and bravery made me vicious. But, oh ! Tom—if I married you and there came a test and you failed me, if you were a coward, I should despise you—I couldn't help it. I'd far rather you'd be bad and brave than good and cowardly— that is, I could love you that way, and I couldn't the other. But you — you're so cautious, so careful, you hate so to run any risk—when we go to places you won't do anything—you hate adventures so—you seem so bound up in your old business—so fussy and particular about details—like an old maid. Oh, it seems to me you aren't manly, and you can't be brave—and it makes me so impatient with you, and then I can't bear you to come near me, and that makes you grieved, and then we are both miserable. No—no—I can't go on—I must be free.''

"You are free," said Tom, quietly. " I have no claim on your heart, and hence none on your hand. And it is better that I should not come here any more ; that we should simply say goodby, and let that end it.''

"I am going away, anyway, soon,'' said Janet, with a touch of sudden feebleness after all her vehemence ; and then, as Tom did not ask where, she went on half absently,

5

" The trip I didn't take with Aunt Elliott last spring I'm to have this spring. Only it's a different trip, of course. Just our own West, all the new States, and anything that seems to be interesting when we get there, without any fixed plan ahead." She mentioned in the same absent way a few of the places they thought of visiting, and wound up with the statement that they should start in about a month.

" A good trip for a romantic young lady. You may see a brave man or two," and Tom smiled pleasantly.

" Oh, Tom, I hate to think of all I've said."

" It was better to say it if it was true."

" But there's so much else that's true. I like you so much. We've been such good friends. Surely you will come here ? I shall see you sometimes ? "

" No. We—well, we should have nothing to talk about for one thing," said Tom, with a little laugh.

" Oh, Tom !—don't ! But tell me—are you—have I—you don't mind very much ? "

" Oh, no," said Tom, cheerfully. " You haven't broken my heart, if that's what you mean. There are plenty of interests left in life. I hate the old business for one thing, and can't bear to spend my whole life in it; and since I haven't got to support a wife I won't. I dare say, too, I shall find travelling more entertaining than matrimony would have been; then we shall agree about one thing at least.''

Janet was nonplussed by his easy way of taking it. '' I'm so glad you feel so about it,'' she said, half-heartedly.

'' Oh, yes, you can relieve your mind of all anxiety on my behalf. To tell the truth,'' he said, '' I'm not sure I wasn't a little bored with being engaged myself; but being a man I hadn't the originality to discover it. Adam let Eve find out things for him, and men ever since have followed his example. Well, I must be going. I hope nothing will interfere with your trip—you're very much to be envied to have such a chance. I hope it will be perfect in every way, and that you'll have lots of fun. I sha'n't see you again, so I'll wish you *bon voyage* now.''

'' Why,'' cried Janet, with wide-open eyes, '' you're saying exactly what you said a year ago—almost word for word.''

'' Am I? That's funny.''

" But you didn't mean it then——"

" Well, I do mean it now," declared Tom, with a smile. " Make my respects to your father and mother, please. Goodby."

Janet stood in the middle of the drawing-room, just where he had taken leave of her, for many minutes. " Doesn't he care at all ? " she asked herself. " Or is it that he cares so much and is too proud to show it ? What if he isn't a coward ? Somehow I haven't liked him so well for months !   I wonder if I can have made a mistake after all ? "

Some instinct of reticence prompted her not to tell her family of what had occurred, but to let them find it out gradually, by ob-servation.

" If Tom Norrie's in here this evening," growled her father, the next night at dinner, " I want to see him."

" I don't expect him to-night," said Janet, quietly.

" Humph ! Thought he was here every night wasting his time. Where is he, then ? "

" I don't know, papa. Why are you so put out with him ? "

" I'm not put out with him. Impudent young jackanapes ! " growled the Bull—but

before he knew it, Miss Janet, by dint of
artful contradictions, sudden agreements and
other tactics, patented by herself for the purpose, had the whole story out of him.

She was awestruck at Tom's new-found
independence, and thrilled, yet half uneasy
over this signal instance of his bravery, for
she knew well what it meant to defy her
father's wrath. But when he did not turn
up the next day at the office, nor the next,
when it was learned that he had drawn a
large sum of money from his bank, and he
was traced as far as Chicago, but utterly lost
from that point on, it began to look to
Janet, as to the others, a very serious matter. It was a genuine and complete disappearance, and she remembered anxiously now
hearing Tom say in days gone by that he
had always thought he should like to disap-
pear—to have the freedom of being practically another person, and to have a new
life as different as possible from any he had
known before.

" If anything happens to him I shall be to
blame," she said to herself, miserably. " I
drove him to it. There's no knowing what
risks he may run—especially if he isn't a
coward ! "— and she spent her days and

many sleepless nights in vain conjecture as to where he had gone, and what he might be doing ; looking forward with feverish eagerness to her own departure for the West, in the forlorn hope that she might somewhere run across him. And as the time passed and there came no word of him, she began to think that she would have to give up everything else to search for him—she was sure that she could find him sooner or later, and this suspense about him was unbearable—it would kill her.

CHAPTER V

A month passed. Tom Norrie spent his first weeks of freedom in travelling from the midwest still westward by such stages, rapid or slow, as suited his mood from day to day. He made friends on the trains with those men whose appearance attracted him most, and sometimes even accompanied these queer acquaintances upon their further journeys. All the conventional social laws that had up to this time regulated his intercourse with other human beings were cast one side. He was hail-fellow with every one, and did not wait to be introduced. Cigars and drinks were introduction enough. They led rapidly to agreeable games of poker, or still more agreeable conversations, in which Mr. Norrie's own engaging frankness about his past career led to equally pleasing confidences on the part of his friend of the moment. Tom invented a plausible yarn of his early life and

adventures, which by dint of frequent repeating began to seem to him so true that
he told it with most convincing verisimili-
tude—suppressing nothing derogatory, nor
yet magnifying unduly those feats of arms
or craft which redounded to his credit.   He
modestly let himself appear as a "tenderfoot," but by accident of circumstance
rather than by temperament, for his tale
showed him no milksop.

In his thirst for real adventure he picked
out wherever he went the most devil-may-
care and reckless faces—those which gave
signs of humor, bravado, and audacity.   He
sought for that character with which he had
invested à priori his Western compatriot ;
he sought to come in closest contact with it,
and then to emulate it.   He found generally, to be sure, peaceful citizens dwelling
behind these brazen masks, and lives com-
monly tame enough beneath the heroic blus-
ter which pleased him.

But again, there was brass within a fair
counterpart to that without, and he found
himself, to his delight, shaking hands and
drinking with gentlemen who if they had
not been in jail belonged there by rights,
and who bragged as lightly of having killed

their man—or possibly several—as Tom
might boast of breaking an unruly horse.
So he sat with them in the gaudy saloons,
and heard their adventures, and narrated his
own imaginary ones, and then followed them
out in quest of those which should be real
and true.   But his search was unrewarded.
He allied himself with these desperate characters, blinked at nothing, talked as loud
and drank as deep as they, went to their
camps or habitations with them, became for
the time one of their gang, friend of their
friends and enemy of their enemies—and
yet, nothing happened.

But he enjoyed more every day the fresh
and racy flavors of the life.   Freedom from
his old bonds was sweet enough, but freedom of this sort put new blood into his
veins.   His manners changed with his fortune, and now the staid city of his birth a
month behind him, only a close observer
would have taken him for anything but a
Westerner of long experience—which, we
may remark parenthetically, does not neces-
sarily mean more than a year.   Out there
time moves more swiftly, and a little of it
goes much farther than in the slower regions
of what we call civilization.   Tom enjoyed

the change so hugely that he hardly gave himself the chance to feel disappointment at the lack of actual events. It was exciting enough at first to be with men of this sort and to be given the freedom, as it were, of their past careers of crime and escape. The escapes were so thrilling that he had thrills himself only to hear them.

And his own transformation into the bold swashbuckler of his imagination pleased him mightily. He took to it all so quickly and so naturally, that there was no effort to him in the rôle. He liked to swagger and talk big. He rather enjoyed the unwonted taste of large oaths in his mouth. He gave his' humor free swing, and found that this raised him high in the esteem of his rough companions. He made them laugh, and then they liked him. His drollery was his passport to favor and grew with the appreciation that it met. He had never earned the reputation of being much of a wag, though he had always himself been amused by his own way of putting things. He enjoyed, perhaps, as much as anything, this sensation of having his jokes appreciated, and liked to feel that he was a good American by inheritance of humor.

As the time drew on he found himself
gravitating back towards the main line of
traffic, from which he had strayed far afield,
and to the region mentioned by Janet as her
first destination in the West, a stage, as it
were, of her journey.   He arrived one evening at the brand-new town of Bud, being
brought thither on a branch line, which
gave him an hour to get his supper at the
Empire Hotel, and to make his connection
with the next train on the other road.   But
when he found the whole little town agog
over a train robbery on the last train up on
the main line, he resolved to stay on until the
next day.   It seemed that the robbery constituted one of a brilliant series which had
dazzled the whole locality in the last month
by their swiftness, effectiveness, and daring.
There was something in the way every one
spoke of the leader of the gang that appealed
powerfully to Tom's imagination.   He was
a young fellow, apparently perfectly fearless,
so nonchalant in the pursuit of his risky
profession, and so easy and humorous in the
treatment of his victims, that instead of being feared and detested, he seemed rapidly
on the way to become a popular idol.   The
waiter at his table regaled Tom with anec-

dotes of him, which, though they were on
the face of them, to even the most credu-
lous hearer, of a legendary and impossible
quality, nevertheless interested Tom more
in their subject with every word. The very
fact that such elaborate and circumstantial
accounts were already current of his recklessness, his bravado, and his chivalry, established in Tom's mind the conviction that
he was an uncommon character, a modern
Robin Hood or Cellini or D'Artagnan—or
a mixture, perhaps, of the three, with the
typical touch of American humor to light-
en and modernize it all. In any event, he
seemed to be the actual embodiment of all
that Tom was seeking, and it was borne in
upon our hero's mind that by hook or by
crook, fair means or dark ones, he must
make this man's acquaintance.

"By George!" he said to himself.
"Why shouldn't I join his gang? There
would be adventure with enough risk to
make any man's heart jump—something
worth coming two or three thousand miles
for! 'It is an honorable kind of thievery,'
besides, and even if I am caught, it's a fellow by some other name that's hanged, not
one of the junior partners in the respectable

house of Norrie, Trumbull & Co.   There's
no one to care what becomes of me, if I
don't bring disgrace on that honored name
—or rather a cloud on its credit.   Janet's
thrown me over—and—well, it would be as
good a way as any to prove that I am not a
coward.   If only it wouldn't involve taking
other people's property !   That was very romantic and proper three or four hundred
years ago—but now, in 1895, somehow it
looks tremendously like stealing.''

With which conflicting reflections, Mr.
Norrie strolled to the bar-room, having ab-
sent-mindedly given his waiter a fee of a
size to cause that person's mouth to fall ajar
and his eyes to goggle with awestruck joy.

'' 'Fraid to risk the trip to-night ? '' inquired the hotel clerk and bartender, when
Tom announced that he should like a room
after all.

'' Afraid—what do you mean ? You don't
think there's any chance of the night train
being held up, do you ? '' asked Tom,
quickly.

'' Well, no—I don't guess there is.   They
don't often hit twice runnin' like that.   But
I thought perhaps you might feel nervous
about night travellin', all the same.''

" I'm no such sissy as that," remarked Mr. Norrie, with easy nonchalance. " On the contrary, I should rather like to meet the gentlemen and observe their methods."

" Reckon you'd not care to meet Tom Nelson more'n once. I've not heard of anybody that was anxious to renew the acquaintance."

" You're mistaken there, Gus," said an elderly smoker across the room. " One o' them gals up from Aurory for the ball—the prettiest one o' the lot, too—was just dead stuck on him. Said he was as polite a gent as she'd ever met, and if 'twarn't for losin' her di'monds she'd like to be held up over agin."

" She's the Sheriff's girl down to Aurory," said another and younger gentleman. " An' she 'bout runs the town herself. You can see her down there any day doin' 'bout as she d—n pleases, an' lookin' pretty's a peach, too. She's got a skin like milk."

The hotel clerk was interested. " You don't mean that stunnin' tall girl in black velvet and a corsij bokay? " he inquired, eagerly.

" That very same," rejoined the previous speaker. " Miss Geraldine Roray; com-

monly called Jerroray—just like they call her
dad the Terror of Aurory—his name bein'
Terrence—and Terroray for short. She
knows how to dress way up, and the Terror
don't think nothin's too good for her. He
made a pile o' plunks off Aurora's boom,
and now she's a spendin' of 'em.''

"Should think she did know how to
dress!" exclaimed the magnificent Augustus. "They ain't a girl in this town can
match the togs she had on to-night. See
here, Neddy Bedloe, will you introjuce me
to her? My time's up in twenty minutes,
and I'm goin' down to the hall for some fun."

"Suppose I want all my own introjuc-
tions myself?" retorted Neddy, sarcastically. "Suppose I'm goin' to have some
fun, too?"

"But you don't dance."

"Hey—don't I? You wait and see!
Bet she dances with me twice to once with
you," said Mr. Bedloe. "I ain't got to
wait twenty minutes till my time's up,"—
with which he rose and went off grinning,
partly at his own cleverness and partly at
the discomfiture of the elegant Augustus, a
gentleman who roused affection in no one's
bosom.

" Bet your friend loses his wager," said Tom, in an ingratiating manner, perceiving his opportunity at this juncture. " A young lady of so much taste as he ascribes to this one doesn't want to circumnavigate a dance-hall with a gentleman who gets himself up in that style. How would he look embracing any black velvet gown and corsij bokay, I should like to know? "

Gus laughed with great cordiality. " Say, you know what's what. Come along with me, and we'll cut Neddy Bedloe out. She's a daisy of a girl."

" I'm your man," said Tom, shaking hands energetically with his new friend. " The young lady sounds interesting, and I look forward to making her acquaintance."

" You'll have to look out for Charley Shore," remarked a man who had not spoken before. " She's his gal."

" Who's Charley Shore? " inquired Gus, contemptuously.

" Feller down to Aurory."

" I'll wager even that she ain't no feller's gal yet," said the humorous elderly smoker who had first brought the young lady into the discussion. " She don't look like it, an' she don't ac' like it. The feller that come

up with her, if that's Mr. Shore, he jus' stood
by as tame as any kitten an' heard her talk
about Tom Nelson. She said as how Tom
had more spunk in his little finger than most
any man she'd ever seed in his whole body—
an' she admired a man that could hold up
trains like he could, four times runnin' in
three weeks, an' scare all Risin' Sun County
an' all Creesote, too, out o' their boots. An'
she specified further if ever she was such a
plumb idiot as to marry any man, she'd look
out she got one as smart as him—or else one
smart enough to get her her dimond neck-
liss back agin—she warn't agoin' to set up
housekeepin' with no hundred - an' - sixty-
pound baby, not she," and the reporter of
this vivacious conversation smiled with evident relish at the recollection of its emphasis.

"She's engaged to Charley Shore, anyhow," stated that gentleman's champion.

"Bein' engaged don't count much with
gals nowadays," replied the man of wisdom.
"They take it like tryin' on hats to the
milliner's—you've got to see lots before you
get one that suits."

"You seem to think you know a lot about
women, Swinney," remarked the hotel clerk,
coldly.

6

" Well, an' hadn't I oughter ? " retorted Mr. Swinney, good-naturedly. "Buried my fourth last month, an' all my mother-in-laws livin', and got six daughters o' my own, an' three sons married to boot—you can just bet I've had some experience with the sex."

" Has this same man really held up four trains in three weeks ? " asked Tom, wishing to get back to the previous question.

" Well, an' where have you been that you don't know it ? " inquired Mr. Swinney, suspiciously.

" This gentleman has only just arrived here by train, an' can't be expected to be familiar with all our local news," said the hotel clerk. " You haven't registered, by the way," he added to Tom, pushing the open book towards him.

Tom signed without a moment's hesitation, " J. Chance, Burr Oak, Nebraska."

" Glad to make your acquaintance, Mr. Chance," said Gus, cordially. " My name's Dicker—Augustus B. Dicker."

Tom rejoined with equal cordiality, and then Mr. Dicker excused himself to make his toilet for the ball, his place being taken by a scrawny boy.

"Local news," murmured Mr. Swinney, as if to himself, "Gus Dicker's crazy. These here train robberies are a national disgrace. They ain't nobody oughter be ignorant of 'em—let alone any traveller what has his life in his hands."

"Well if you enlighten me, Mr. Swinney," said Tom, with engaging candor, "then I shall no longer be ignorant."

This view of the matter appeared to appeal to Mr. Swinney, and he forthwith narrated all that was known of the train robberies which had so upset Rising Sun and Creosote Counties and alarmed the whole State.

A gang of masked men, computed to number anywhere from fifteen to thirty, led by the soft-voiced and gentlemanly desperado who had won Miss Roray's admiration, had terrorized train after train, met with no resistance whatever from train-crews or passengers, and carried off large booty. They seemed to have mysterious means of information, for in each case there had been consignments of gold in the express-cars. Quantities of both money and valuables also had been taken from the passengers. It was generally estimated that in the three previous hauls the robbers had secured something

like $150,000, and this last raid had brought
them good treasure trove.   The attacks had
followed each other in such rapid succession
that people had hardly had time to realize
what was happening and to take action upon
it.   The sheriffs, whether they were paralyzed
by fright, which was not a likely hypothesis
in the case of Aurora's Terror, or had been
purchased by Mr. Nelson, which was even
less likely, at all events did not stir themselves.   There were forts full of soldiers
within short distance, but it was not easy
to set in motion the unwieldy and rust covered machine that should in the end order
them into the field.   Moreover, the difficulties in the way of accomplishing anything
were enormous.   A handful of outlaws could
shift about with the greatest ease—strike
here, strike there—and be off before their
pursuers could know where they were, much
less attack them.

    " 'Taint the millingtary nor the perlice
that's wanted—it's public opinion," stated
Mr. Swinney.   "Those men lives somewheres, and they gets food, and some folks
knows something about 'em, sure.   But
they ain't nobody that's willin' to let on.
In fact, they do it so awful cute that some-

how people seem to be pleased by it, so long
as they don't lose no money themselves.
And there's actually some folks, like this
here Jerroray from Aurory, that even 'pears
to take pride in Tom Nelson an' his goin's
on. Which I may say I can't sympathize
with."

"P'raps if you'd met him, like me, you
would sympathize," said a gaunt ranchman
in a red flannel shirt and long boots, shift-
ing his quid with some embarrassment as all
eyes turned upon him.

"An' then agin, perhaps I wouldn't,"
retorted Mr. Swinney, with scorn.

"What was your experience?" asked
Tom with eager interest.

"I's on the last train he held up afore
this one, and when he come to me, says I to
him, 'Tom Nelson,' says I, 'I'm a poor
farmer,' says I, 'an' if you want my last
plunk you can have it, but my woman'll
have to go 'thout her new dress an' the kid
won't get no go-cart. I reckon he'll cry,'
says I, 'but here's ten dollars if you've got
to have it,' says I. Gentlemen, Tom Nelson he handed over to me a ten dollar bill
outen his own pocket, he did. 'Keep your
plunks,' says he, 'and take this to buy yer

kid a go-cart and anything else he'd like as
a present from Tom Nelson. An' I most
cleaned out the store up here to Bud, an'
that kid he knows where it all comes from,
an' you can bet Tom Nelson he ain't got
no enemies to our house.''

"I heard he said he didn't want no
workin' man's cash, nohow,'' said another
smoker.

" An' I've heard that he haint never took
no cash from coves what lives in Risin' Sun
County or Creosote,'' said a fourth.

"How about these young ladies' dimond
rings an' bracelets an' necklises, comin' up
from Aurory to the ball to-night ? '' inquired
Mr. Swinney, with sarcastic inflection.

"Dimonds ain't money, an' you heard
'em all say as how he give 'em back their
purses, an' said he warn't the gent to deprive
a lady of her travellin' expenses.''

"Awful polite to give ladies back four or
five mean little dollars, when he's tuck jewels
worth a couple o' hundred or so,'' was Mr.
Swinney's comment.

"Jewels is luxuries, he says,'' remarked
number three. "An' I agree with him.
Anybody as can afford dimonds, an' keep
'em out o' hock, too, for wearin' purposes,

ain't exactly poverty struck, an' it ain't
agoin' to break 'em to pay toll to Tom Nelson.   Tom Nelson don't want to break nobody."

"The poor man's friend?" suggested
Tom Norrie.

"Exactly!" shouted Mr. Swinney.
"You've hit it, Mr. Chance.   He's the
poor man's friend, which no household
should be without him!   What did I tell
yer 'bout these folks bein' on his side?
They ain't one of them here that'd join a
posse to catch Tom Nelson.   I'm even
thinkin' they'd fight on his side, stid of
aginst him.   None of 'em seems to recolleck
that he ain't no more'n a common thief."

"Ain't no common thief about Tom Nelson," declared one champion.

"He's a gentleman, Tom Nelson is, an'
that's more'n you can say o' some folks what
ain't thieves," said another.

"Tom Nelson don't hurt us, an' we ain't
goin' to hurt him till he does," declaimed
the third.   "He don't burgle our banks nor
our stores.   He don't bleed the farmer nor
tech the upright citizen.   He don't want to
scare our wives nor our kids, an' he'll keep
on lettin' us alone just as long as we let him

alone.   But if we try muxin' with his business they ain't no tellin' what he might do
to our'n.   Thief or no thief I'm for lettin'
of him alone an' keepin' on the good side of
him.''   This eloquent statement of the case
was followed by a little murmur of approval,
even from those that had at first seemed to
side with the strictures of Mr. Swinney.

    '' None of you ain't got no patriotism,''
said that gentleman in disgust.   '' These
train robberies is a disgrace to the State an'
to the whole country.''

    '' Patriotism oughter begin at home, like
charity an' them things,'' retorted the leader
of the majority.   '' An' I guess we'll feel satisfied with ourn if Risin' Sun and Creosote
Counties gets out of it with whole skins.''

    This sentiment was applauded warmly,
and Tom Norrie's interest in Tom Nelson
grew with the signs of his popularity.

    '' You fellers'll be sending Mr. Nelson to
Congress next,'' he remarked.   '' Nobody
would have half a chance against him.   I
believe you'll make him President of the
United States before you've done with him.''

    The majority and minority both grinned
at this idea, but Tom's further questions
about the personality and methods of the

outlaw were cut short by the appearance of
Mr. Dicker in full ball regalia. He wore
the regulation swallow-tail coat, with gray
trousers in a heavy stripe, a white piqué
waistcoat cut high, a straight collar cut
higher, and a four-in-hand tie of pale blue
satin.   By way of further decorations he had
on, of course, his diamond pin, a watch-
chain and charms festooned about the white
piqué façade, and several magnificent rings.

" Whew ! '' said Tom, at sight of this resplendent vision ; '' if your town here's a
bud, I should say you were the full-blown
blossom ! ''

Everybody laughed again, but Mr. Dicker,
conscious of his superlatively fine appearance, was only flattered by these demonstrations, and swelled visibly at the plaudits of
his townsmen.

" I'll have to make a pretty big bluff at
Miss Roray, if I'm going to get her eyes off
you,'' remarked Tom, further ; and he and
Mr. Dicker made their exit amid renewed
gayety, while the whole assembly adjourned
to the ball-room to see the fun.

CHAPTER VI

There were many pretty girls at the ball, but " Jerroray " was easily the prettiest and easily the belle of the occasion. She was a fine tall creature, of magnificent physical development, with a waist so small in comparison with her full hips and swelling bust that the alarmed spectator was perforce led to wonder what she did with her inside anatomy. There was surely not room within that slender zone of velvet for the necessary machinery to keep so much bloom still blooming. Tom Norrie regarded it with awe, and wondered, as most men do, why women should consider such deformity beautiful. But the attractions of Miss Roray's head being superlative, he did not look long at these exaggerations of her figure. She possessed a quantity of blonde hair, done up in a great pointed knob high at the back, decorated lavishly with gold pins, and finished

off with the usual thick fuzz around the
face. But her eyes were so large and clear,
her skin so dazzlingly white, her neck and
shoulders so splendid, that even this vulgar
and inartistic coiffure could not spoil her,
as it spoils so many merely pretty women.
And beneath the blonde fuzz that veiled
her forehead was the saving grace of dark,
straight eyebrows, which seemed to Tom
the means of rescuing her countenance from
the class of the colorless blonde, and invest-
ing it at once with a quality of vividness,
and even daring, that he found wonderfully
attractive.

But the young lady's demeanor was not at
all that of daring and pride. She did not
hold her head particularly high, nor did she
often toss it. She appeared to be having an
extraordinarily good time, and she didn't in
the least mind showing it. This childlike
air of naïve jollity seemed to Tom curiously
out of keeping both with her really splendid
beauty and with the magnificent simplicity of her attire. Her trained black velvet
fitted her superbly, its plainness showing
every line of her figure. The bodice was
cut extremely low, and the great puffs of the
sleeves were caught up to conceal as little as

possible of the round, white arm.   The only
relief in the severity of the gown came in
the heavy white lace around the open neck,
and in a great bunch of bluish purple flow-
ers, which lay upon the bosom as if half to
cover the dazzling display permitted by the
low lines of the bodice.   It was a costume
fit for a duchess, a costume that indicated
the dignity of pride and high-breeding, that
would have been appropriate to Miss Roray
had she been twice the age she seemed
(" by George," said Tom to himself, " what
a stunner she'll be at forty—five times as
good looking as she is now ! ")—and that
was singularly inappropriate to the easy manners and the romping merriment with which
she played her part in the festivities of the
evening.

" I'll be d—d if she ain't the stunningest
girl I ever laid eyes on," said Mr. Dicker,
in a tone of suppressed enthusiasm.   " Glad
I put on all my own clothes," he added, regarding himself with fond pride before he
sallied forth to conquer.

But in spite of the quantity of clothes he
had put on, and all the lavish adornments of
his person, Mr. Dicker did not conquer ; nor
yet did Mr. Neddy Bedloe ; and Mr. Charley

Shore himself, donor of the large solitaire diamond which had decorated Miss Roray's finger until it was removed by the train robber this very night, even Mr. Charley Shore was minus the extra privileges of an engaged man which had lately accrued to his share. All these gentlemen were entirely cast into the shade by a newcomer, and this favored stranger was, to Tom's own surprise and everyone else's, the gentleman who was introduced as Mr. Chance, of Nebraska. '

Tom's costume was anything but metropolitan; like Mr. Bedloe, he had added no embellishments for the occasion. Jerroray scarcely noticed him as he was led up to her to be presented by his elegant friend, the hotel clerk. But from the moment Tom began speaking to her, explaining his special interest in making her acquaintance through her reported interest in Mr. Nelson, the outlaw, the young lady gave him an undivided and complete attention. She looked bewildered, puzzled, questioning, and her fine brows drew closer together than ever in a frown of perplexity.

"Say, you ain't from this vicinity, are you?" she inquired after a minute, interrupting what he was saying.

Tom admitted that he was not.

" Then where 've I seen you before ? "

Tom, being confident that she had never seen him before, was unable to conjecture where.

" Well, you're mighty familiar to me somehow. I don't know whether you favor any of my friends or not, but anyhow seems as if I'd known you ever so long.——You seem so natural, somehow," she continued, regarding him closely. " Don't he seem so to you, Charley ? Don't he seem awful natural ? " she inquired of Mr. Shore.

That gentleman somewhat gruffly couldn't say that he did, couldn't say that there was anything familiar to him in the appearance or manners of Mr. Chance.

" Well, he seems awful natural to me," repeated Miss Roray. " Awful nice, too," she added, with a little laugh. " I can't recolleck who you remind me of, but I know it's somebody I liked," she declared with artless candor.

" You are very flattering," said Tom, with an elegant bow, quite out of keeping with the character he had assumed in the name of Chance. Then, the music striking up, he covered his blushes by begging for a waltz, and Miss Roray, coolly requesting Charley "to excuse her," granted him the favor.

Now Tom, in the season of his courtship of Janet Trumbull, had become an expert dancer, and finding that he had an excellent partner, he dropped at once into his favorite rhythmical, smooth glide. It pleased him that the young lady should appreciate this poetry of motion to the extent of not spoiling it with attempts at conversation.

" My, but you just know how to waltz ! " she declared when the music stopped. " They ain't a man in this room can do it like that. Where'd you learn ? "

" The other side of the Mississippi River," said Tom, with a smile.

Jerroray smiled, too. " You ain't goin' to tell me anything you don't want me to know, are you ? " she inquired, shrewdly.

" Ah ! " said Tom. " Do you think I could conceal from you anything that you cared to know about my insignificant self ? Speak the word and I lay before you my whole history."

She looked puzzled for a moment, then again broke into her easy smile. " Say, you

ain't no such chump as that ! I know better ;
you're talkin' through your hat ! "

"Well, if you don't want my history
you needn't have it—especially if you'll
tell me your experiences with the train robber.   I understand you took quite a fancy
to him."

" I should just guess ! " said Miss Roray,
with emphasis.   " Say, he was a real gentleman, now, an' you wouldn't expect that of
a highway robber, would you ?   I can tell
you, it just knocked me flat."

" Er—how did he show it exactly ? "

" Well, I'll tell you.   It was this way.
Me'n Charley was discussin' the situation.
I had all my diamonds with me, an' of
course I just hated to lose 'em, so I says to
Charley, ' I'm goin' to ask him to let me
have 'em back,' says I.   An' Charley he
sat there shiverin' like a mould o' jelly, an'
says he, ' If you ain't a d—n fool, Geraldine, you'll keep your mouth shut for once,
unless you want your head blowed off.'   An'
that made me mad, an' I says to Charley,
says I, ' Charley Shore, nothin' ever gave
you any right to call me names or swear at
me, even if you are scared blue, an',' says I,
' I shall do as I like,' says I.   So when Tom

Nelson got up to us I smiles at his old black mask just as sweet as I knows how.''

" It's uncommonly sweet, too,'' declared Tom, with a sigh, " much too sweet for a train robber ! "

" Get along,'' said Miss Roray, elegantly. "An' says I to him, ' Mr. Nelson,' says I, ' here's all my diamonds,' says I ; ' if you want to rob a poor girl who never did you no harm, but I'm likely to have a pretty poor sort of a husband to support one o' these days,'—pointin' over my shoulder to Charley, sittin' there awful glum an' scared—an' there'll come a time when our last crust'll be gone, an' I shall want 'em awful bad to put 'em up with my uncle, an' get some good, solid plunks in exchange—else I'll have to take in washin', ' says I. ' You wouldn't want me to take in washin', would you, Mr. Nelson ? ' An' he touched his hat like a gentleman soon's I spoke to him, the man behind a-keepin' everybody else's hands up all the time, an' he a-drawin' on me, an' now he began laffin' as if he was awful pleased ; an' says he, ' My dear young lady,' says he—them was his exact words—' I'll have to take your diamonds now, but perhaps you'll see 'em again some day, an' if

you do,' says he, ' think of me.   An' let me
give you a little piece of advice,' says he, ' if
it ain't takin' too great a liberty.'   ' Not at
all,' says I ; ' advise ahead.'   ' Well,' says
he, ' don't be in too much of a hurry to
marry, an' when you do finally take the fatal
step, look out to get a man who'll not let
your diamonds be took away from you.'   An'
then, all smilin,' he took Charley's things,
Charley bein' as mad as hops, but forkin'
'em all over as meek's Pike's Peak.   An'
says I, ' Oh ! I forgot my hairpins ; ' an' says
he, ' Let 'em alone ; they look too attractive
to be disturbed.'   An' he wouldn't take my
purse nor any of the girls', an' for my part
I think he's just an elegant outlaw, and I'd
like awful well to meet him again—now,
wouldn't you ? ''

 " Well—I don't quite know,'' laughed
Tom.   '' Of course, not being an attractive
young lady—— ''

 '' Oh, I mean if you was me.   Somehow
I never dreamed Tom Nelson would be like
that.   I sort o' expected he'd be harsh with
me, like Charley said, and tell me to hold
my gab ; but my ! you don't often meet a
politer young gent.   Say, don't you think it
would be fun to be a highway robber or a

pirate, or somethin' of that sort ?   Seems to
me it's awful romantic.''

" It would be just immense fun,'' said
Tom, with genuine enthusiasm.   '' If you
could only have the risk and the excitement
without being a thief, I'd join Tom Nelson's
gang to-morrow.''

'' Say, you're a peach !   Shake ! '' and
this engaging young woman held out her
hand with an enthusiasm that matched his
own.   It was a fine large hand, such as suited
the generous proportions of its owner, and
there was nothing coy or squeamish in its
frank, warm grasp.

Messrs. Dicker, Bedloe, Shore & Co. observed this passage of hands with rage in
their hearts, and at a later day Tom had
cause to regret the enmity so innocently
earned.   But he was really not monopolizing
Jerroray any more than she was monopolizing him ; and at all events they were both so
absorbed that they were happily unaware of
the malevolent glances that fell upon them.

'' You know I like a man that's got some
spunk,'' continued Miss Roray, explaining
her impulse while her hand was still in
Tom's.   '' To tell the plain truth, I'm gettin' awful sick of Charley Shore.   Funny,

too, when it warn't two months ago I was
dreadful stuck on him ! I know why well
enough, too. He's sort of a pretty feller,
an' he looked so kind o' nice and mannish
in his dress suit, an' then there was somethin' awful fascinatin' 'bout the way he ·
smoked cigarettes. I used to watch him light
'em and then puff away so easy, an' think I
wouldn't mind a bit havin' him try to kiss
me, though I always slapped the other fellers.
So when he popped I said ' Yes,' though my
dad told me I was an awful fool—an' Terence was right, too, an' I'll tell him so when
I go home to-morrer. But I can't give
Charley back his ring," she added, with her
little laugh. " He'll have to ask Tom Nelson for that ! "

" Poor Mr. Shore ! " said Tom. " Is his
fate sealed ? Has it all happened in a day,
or had the course of love been checkered
previously ? "

" Oh, well, we've quarrelled a lot, of
course, because Charley's awful exactin', an'
I've been brought up to do as I please, an'
no questions asked. I couldn't stand his
interferin' way, an' give him notice to quit
long ago, but I don't know's I thought I
shouldn't marry him until to-night. Some-

how, if there's anything in the world I hate
it's a coward, an' I can't get over his sittin'
there, in a blue funk like, an' handin' his
things over to Tom Nelson just as cheap's
dirt, an' never sayin' a word ! I tell you he
didn't look very pretty then, an' I can't
make it seem that he ever will look pretty
to me again ! "

" He couldn't very well have resisted Mr.
Nelson," said Tom, in a spirit of fairness,
remembering how his own engagement had
been broken on similar grounds. Were
women all alike after all? Did his dark,
fascinating Janet, highly educated and re-
fined as she was, think and feel like this extraordinary flower of Western civilization?
But he hadn't much time for reflection, for
Jerroray was replying with voluble sarcasm
to his defence of her *fiancé*, and he had to
listen and laugh.

"Oh, no," she said. "Of course he
couldn't very well resist—that's what all the
men think—poor scared little dears !—an' so
Mr. Tom Nelson has his way with us, an'
ropes in the plunks an' the diamonds. I
look pretty without my necklace, don't I?"

" You do, indeed," declared Tom, with
sincerity.

" It's nice, ain't it, to go to a ball without any jewels? No bracelets, no pins, no
decorations of any sort—I tell you I feel
about half dressed. An' you needn't let on
to me that if any one man on a train had the
spunk to get up an' make a stand some of
the rest wouldn't help him, an' they couldn't
clean out the train robbers in less time than
it takes to tell it. No, sir, I know better.
They say Tom Nelson's got a great big gang ;
but he had only one man in our car to keep
hands held up, an' one to watch the engineer and fireman, an', so far as heard from,
one other watchman who was poppin' away
outside to keep the folks scared. Now, of
course, there may have been twenty men
round the train, but that's all anybody saw
or knew about, an' I'll bet you even that
he ain't got in all more'n six men to help
him. My theory about Tom Nelson is that
he's puttin' up a great big bluff, an' if any
of these tame lambs round here that call
'emselves men had any spunk at all they could
just call his hand and show him up. But
there ain't one that's a match for him—an'
that's what I like about him, an' don't like
about your Shores and your Dickers an' your
this and thats. I like men an' not sheep."

"I'm sure the men would reciprocate, if there were any," said Tom.

"Well, now," declared the young lady, "you're what I call a man. You could see the fun in bein' a train robber, an' you'd like to hold up trains yourself, but when I asked Charley Shore, he just turned up his nose awful pious, an' says he, 'No man as is a man could ever do anything so low an' dishonest—common thievin' it is an' no more.' An' says I to him, 'No man as is a sheep, which, it seems to me, you all are round here, would ever dare do anything so gritty an' smart. You'd be scared out o' your lives an' funk it all.' An' then says he, 'Geraldine' (when he calls me Geraldine that means he's mad), 'you're crazy,' an' says I to him, 'Charles, you're a timid little babe.' An' then we stopped talkin', an' I've only danced with him once to-night, an' to-morrer he'll get the mitten."

"Poor Mr. Shore," said Tom, with feeling ; then added, gallantly, "but the world's the gainer.

"The world?" queried Miss Roray, puzzled.

"The other men who were left before to

envy Mr. Shore his luck," explained Tom.
" Now we all have a chance ! "

" Oh," said Jerroray, " you meant that ? "
Then she turned her big gray eyes squarely
into his for a moment, with a look which
was much more of curious scrutiny and con-
sideration than of coquetry. " Well," she
remarked, finally, " if you call it a chance,
all I can say is that the man who gets me
back my diamonds will have about all there
is of it."

" You mean that ? " said Tom.

" You bet," she replied, briefly. " I always mean what I say. An' I'm pretty
safe on this, because it'll take considerable
more'n any chump to beat Tom Nelson."

" That's true enough," said Tom.
" You've given us a magnificent chance—a
chance in the first place to prove we aren't
chumps, and in the second place to win a
splendid reward for not being chumps."

" But suppose you don't any of you get
'em, what'll I do then ? " inquired Miss
Roray, with great seriousness.

" That is a predicament which I can't
contemplate with equanimity," returned
Mr. Norrie, with equal gravity.

" I know ; I'll hunt up Tom Nelson and

set my cap for him!" cried the young lady. "You know I don't think it would be half bad fun to marry a train robber. It would be an awful excitin' life—you'd never get bored and wish you'd married some more entertainin' gent."

"If you talk that way I shall become an outlaw at once in good earnest," declared Tom.

Jerroray emitted her pleased little laugh. "Say, you're awful nice. Wish I could think who you remind me of."

"Oh, don't bother about that; it just wastes time in which you might be thinking of me directly, if you would deign to be so very kind and flattering," and Tom bowed humbly.

"I'll bet you've got another girl somewhere that you like better'n me, for all your fine speeches," said Miss Roray, shrewdly. "Hain't you, now? Well, you needn't look at me like that, or Charley Shore'll bite your head off. Goodness gracious, what a lot of time I've been spendin' on you anyhow! How many dances have we missed? Come, I must be hustlin' round an' gettin' my card worked off."

"You must give me some more dances,"

said Tom, trying to get possession of the much pencilled card which she brandished before him.

"No, siree, Chance — not just now. You've had enough for the present. But later on in the evenin' we'll talk about it, an' if you take a shine to go down to Aurory with me to-morrer mornin', I'll undertake to make you have a bang-up good time."

"Agreed," said Tom. "I was going anyway, but I'm all the more glad to be invited, and if I'm to be your knight and look up your property, you've got to fit me out with your colors, power of attorney, and other trifles of that nature."

"Not much," retorted Miss Roray. "If you can't do it on your own hook you'll get no help from me." And she blew him a saucy kiss as she waltzed away on the arm of Mr. Augustus Dicker, who glowered blackly at Mr. Chance, as, indeed, he had been doing industriously for half an hour or more, in company with several other gentlemen, who shared his grievance.

"Well," said Tom to himself, here's my chance for an adventure at last, and I couldn't ask for a better ! A youthful pirate, who is at the same time a popular idol, to

be encountered in the gallant behalf of a
young lady, who talks slang and bad gram-
mar, yet dresses like a duchess and is as
handsome a woman as I've ever seen—yes,
handsomer than Janet even. . . . But,
suppose I secure the diamonds—and she falls
on my neck for gratitude? A man might do
worse than marry so engaging a young person—but—do I want to marry? And am I
fitted to make the fair Jerroray happy?''

He laughed spontaneously at the thought
of such a matrimonial joke, and the ladies
and gentlemen in the vicinity stared at his
solitary merriment.

'' But when a hero begins to reflect he
ceases to be a hero,'' went on Mr. Norrie ;
''and if I'm going in for this adventure I
must take it as it comes, a day at a time,
and let the future attend to itself. If the
young lady elects to marry me, I must meet
my fate like a man—and surely it would be
difficult to find a more entertaining life companion. So hurrah for the blooming West !
Three cheers for Tom Nelson ! Jerroray forever ! '' And in excellent humor with himself and the world about him, Mr. Norrie
proceeded to enter into the festivities of the
evening with a zest which made him an im-

mediate favorite with all the young women, and an object of envy and admiration with most of the young men. The gaudy, gilded lodge-room, the queer customs of the society in which he found himself, the peculiar notions of dress and manners, were all sources of pleasure to our hero, and his delight was crowned by the evident partiality evinced towards him increasingly, as the night wore on, by the blooming Geraldine.

CHAPTER VII

As Tom came into the bar-room the next morning after breakfast, Mr. Dicker and his allies of the foregoing evening responded but coldly to his greetings. A young man, tall and slight, somewhat of Tom's own build, was leaning on the bar and turning over the leaves of the hotel register, and as Tom said good - morning to Mr. Dicker this young man looked up quickly, and regarded our hero with a pair of very keen, dark eyes, during the colloquy that followed.

Tom began by offering Mr. Dicker a cigar, with an urbanity that slightly thawed that gentleman's chilly demeanor.

" I say, Dicker, what time does the morning train go to—to Bloomer ? "

" Ten o'clock," replied Mr. Dicker. " Are you a-goin' to Bloomer ? " he then inquired, with a touch of suspicion in his voice.

"I am contemplating that trip," was Tom's reply.

"Thought you might prefer stoppin' off at Aurory," remarked the hotel clerk, sarcastically, with a wink at the gallery behind Tom.

Tom looked perfectly innocent. "Is Aurora much of a place — worth stopping at?" he asked.

"Depends on whether you're interested in its products," and Mr. Dicker laughed in a suggestive manner.

"Seems to produce very pretty girls," said Tom, coolly. "What else? Is there a good hotel—as good as this?"

"The Empire Hotel is the best this side of Bloomer," declared Mr. Dicker, proudly. "But the Palace down at Aurory is fair. Proprietor's a chump; he's his own clerk and general manager, and don't even know how to dress—but the house is decent."

"I say, Dicker, you've got so much taste in dress, why don't you publish a bulletin to give points to us fellers that's less gifted? 'Bud's Monthly Blossom' you could call it, with your own portrait in your newest costume on the front page of every issue. I've knocked about a good deal, but I never saw a man dressed the way you were last night. Hope you don't mind being copied, for I propose to go and get some togs like 'em.''

This was delivered so coolly and naturally that Mr. Dicker could not suspect that game was being made of him. He fell neatly into the trap of flattery, and expatiated on his views of dress, to the evident pleasure of the other young man as well as of Tom Norrie.

" Let me make you acquainted with Mr. Potts, Mr. Chance," said the hotel clerk, as Mr. Potts evinced a desire to enter into the conversation. He coughed and cleared his throat, and his voice, when he did speak, was very hoarse and thick.

" Jack Potts, representing the firm of Finkstein, Moses & Levi, leading wholesale jewellers, of Chicago, at your service," he said in a tone which, in spite of the unattractive voice, suggested somehow to Tom that all life was a good joke, and prepossessed him at once in Mr. Potts's favor.

" And a very popular gent wherever he goes," supplemented Mr. Dicker.

" Jack-pots generally are popular," rejoined Mr. Potts, easily.

Tom, on further scrutiny, was thoroughly

pleased with the looks of his new acquaintance, and laughed cordially at this witti-
cism as he shook hands with him.   But just
at that moment, hearing a rustle of skirts in
the hall beyond, and catching a glimpse of
Jerroray on her way to the dining-room, he
begged to be excused and hurried after her,
followed by many malevolent glances.

" Who is he ? " inquired Jack Potts at
once, in a confidential undertone, with a
look of the deepest interest on his keen and
clever face.

" No good," rejoined the sapient Mr.
Dicker.   " Turned up here last night—never
saw him before."

" What time last night ? "

" Nine o'clock or so."

" Where from ? "

" Said he came up on the Red Gulch
Road.   Didn't say where from.   Not a com-
municative gent."

Jack Potts shrugged his shoulders.   " Perhaps he has good reason."

" What do you mean ? " asked Mr.
Dicker, eagerly.

" Oh, nothin'.   He seems a good fellow
'nough—but somehow—well—he struck me
as a bit shady.   Can't think who he reminds

me of," went on Mr. Potts, in a puzzled tone.
" Where'd he register from ? "

" Some backwoods place in Nebraska,"
said Mr. Dicker.   " Say, you seem to be
catchin' cold ? "

Jack Potts, without answering, but suppressing a cough, turned to the name in the
register.   " ' J. Chance,' " he said.   " ' Burr
Oak, Nebraska.'   He's no more from Nebraska than I am.   He's an Easterner.
' Chance,'—that's a queer name.—Who'd
he go out to see just now ? " he questioned,
suddenly.

" Jerry Roray, a silly little flirt up from
Aurory, that he met at the ball last night."

" Oh, he went to the ball ? "

" I was fool enough to take him," said
Mr. Dicker.   " He'n this girl got stuck on
each other right off.   Stunnin' lookin' girl—
dressed way up—but an awful fool.   Lost
her diamonds an' things on the train up
here last night, but took just as much pride
in Tom Nelson as if she was his best girl.
An' this little Chance he sailed in and piled
up the gush on Tom Nelson, and so she
thinks he's as brave as a lion, and every
other man a coward, and dances with him
most all night.   He had on just them same

8

clothes he's wearin' this mornin', too; you wouldn't suppose a girl'd look at him, but he's cute, he is," said Mr. Dicker, bitterly.

"Gushed about Tom Nelson, did he?" queried Jack Potts. "What did he say?"

"Oh, a lot of rot; asked all sorts of questions about him; let on he'd never even heard of these train robbers; said Nelson must be a smart cuss, an' he wouldn't mind bein' a train robber himself if it weren't for the thievin'. That's what took Jerry Roray. She thought he must be awful brave to talk like that. Bet you if Mr. Chance ever met Tom Nelson he'd cut an' run for his life."

"You don't like him?"

"He talks too much to suit me. Lays it on too thick," explained Mr. Dicker.

"Wish I could remember who he reminds me of," said Jack Potts again. "Or else I've seen him before somewheres. I have it—it's his voice! He talks for all the world like Tom Nelson himself!"

"You don't say!" exclaimed Mr. Dicker. "You was in that first hold up, warn't you? Come here that night?"

"Yes," said Jack Potts. "Of course Nelson was masked. He was a tall, slight

feller—pretty much the same figure as this
Chance of Nebraska.   I noticed his voice
particularly, for I saw that was about all he
could be identified by, and I'll be d——d
if this feller don't talk just like him.   Say,
if he's goin' down to Aurora, guess I'll go
on the same train and keep an eye on him.
He strikes me as rather interestin'.   I'll just
hustle out and finish up my business here in
a hurry.''

Whereupon Mr. Potts went out on the
street at once in haste, leaving Mr. Dicker
agog with unjust suspicions, in regard to our
hero.   Nor was he slow in sharing them
with Mr. Shore, Mr. Bedloe, and other ag-
grieved parties of the night before, whose
curiosity had been greatly roused by the bits
they had caught of Mr. Potts's discreet conversation.

So when Tom, escorting Miss Roray, took
the ten o'clock train down from Bud, he
was, as the dime novels would put it, a
marked man, though he, in his innocence,
thought the unkind glances directed at him
were all to be charged to Jerroray's account.
But he found himself so fascinated by that
young lady's genial frankness of demeanor,
and so content in her society, that these un-

pleasant signs and portents had no deterrent effect upon him. He would have monopolized her all the way to Aurora had she permitted, and she might have permitted but for some occurrences not planned for or expected.

Miss Roray's appetite was excellent, and she had lingered so long over the breakfast table with Tom chatting beside her that they nearly missed the train. When they entered it all the seats upon the shady side were taken. Tom nodded to Mr. Jack Potts as he passed him, occupying alone one of these more desirable seats, and then placed his fair companion in the full sunshine a little back on the opposite side. Mr. Shore, Mr. Bedloe, and other well known gentlemen from Aurora, some accompanied by their ladies, and some alone, glowered at them, each from his own separate shady seat, up and down the car, but offered not to rise.

"Polite, ain't they?" observed Jerroray, audibly. "I do admire their manners! —— Who was that gent you bowed to comin' in?" she asked the next moment, in a lower tone.

"A drummer I met at the hotel," said

Tom. "In the jewelry business. Jack Potts by name."

"Jolly name—sounds as gamy as he looks."

"I thought his way of looking at you a little too gamy."

"He did give me a pretty steady eye," replied Jerroray, complacently, "but a girl don't mind that—so long as there's nothin' disrespec'ful in it. If a man don't know her it's his way of sayin' he likes her looks, an' every girl likes her looks liked."

"You're all sad flirts, in other words," observed Tom, "and the prettier you are the worse flirts. I'm afraid the lucky dog that gets your diamonds for you will enter that day upon a troublous life."

"Well, if you ain't afraid of Tom Nelson guess you needn't be afraid of me," laughed Miss Roray, good-humoredly. At the mention of Tom Nelson's name Jack Potts started and turned quickly, looking in their direction. Now he at once rose and approached Tom, lifting his hat, with a pleasant smile.

"Wouldn't you be able to make your lady-friend more comfortable on the shady side of the car?" he inquired. "You're welcome to my seat."

" Oh, thank you, Potts," said Tom, turning to Miss Roray, to see how she looked
upon the offer.

" That's what I call polite," remarked
that fair lady - friend, emphatically, rising
to make the transit, and suggesting to Tom
that he should introduce the gent.

Tom did so, and Jerroray and Mr. Potts
shook hands with each other before she
passed on into his seat and settled herself
there with great airs of satisfaction. " You
killed two birds with one stone that time,
Mr. Potts," she remarked, in a friendly tone.

" How so ? " he queried, following them
as she had intended.

" You made me your grateful friend forever, and you set a good example to all
these country - jakes, that don't know how
to treat a lady." This remark was plainly
audible to most occupants of the car, and so
was Mr. Potts's ingenious and tactful reply.

" Ah ! you must not judge us too harshly.
Any gentleman here would doubtless have
given you his seat, but to give it to you and
another gentleman—really, Miss Roray, isn't
that a little too much ? "

" But you did it."

" I only saw you first five minutes since.

If it had been ten minutes I can't answer
for what I might have done," and Mr.
Potts bowed gallantly. "Besides, you forget the other bird I killed. I secured an
introduction to you by my wholly disinter-
ested act."

"You drummers have got more face!"
declared Miss Roray, with her little pleased
laugh. "But you do know how to say
things awful cute. You're a drummer, too,
ain't you, Chance?" she asked, drawing
Tom back into the conversation from which
he had felt a trifle left out.

"Does that imply that I, too, say things
awful cute?" asked Tom, amused at her
cleverness, but flattered in spite of himself.

"You've a pretty neat turn to your
tongue, I've noticed, which always reminds
me of the travellin' perfession. These stay-
at-homes down at Aurory, like Charley
Shore for instance, may mean more'n you
fellers do—but they can't say it. They can
feel an awful lot, but stayin' at home don't
make 'em think very quick, somehow," and
the young lady smiled pleasantly at both
young men, as she uttered this Shakespearean
truth to wits that were certainly not home-
keeping.

"I always mean a good deal more than I say," declared Mr. Chance, of Nebraska, gazing eloquently into Miss Roray's eyes.

"And I say what I mean, at least," put in Jack Potts, quickly, "and answer questions, too, when they're asked me by beautiful and discernin' young ladies."

Jerroray laughed. "If that's a hit at Chance it won't have any effect on him," she said. "I've asked him lots of questions, but he's got out of 'em all. He don't intend to give himself away!"

"Prince in disguise, eh?" asked Jack Potts, genially.

"That must be it!" she cried, delighted.

"Wish I could think who you remind me of," said the drummer to Tom; "or else I've seen you before somewhere."

"Say, that's exactly what I feel about him," cried Miss Roray. "Ain't that funny now? It runs in my head all the time, but I can't get hold of it."

"I seem to be a mysterious character," observed Tom. "I can assure you, however, that I've not seen either of you before. Do you imagine I could forget it if I'd ever put my eyes on you?" he asked Miss Roray, impressively.

" I say," said Mr. Potts, " it's your voice. Ain't that it, Miss Roray ? "

" Perhaps it is," she replied, in a puzzled tone. " But I can't think who it's like."

" I can," declared Jack Potts, in a tone so significant that they both quickly looked at him. " His voice is like one that I've heard only once—you've heard it, too, Miss Roray, but you didn't see the man's face— it came from behind a black mask."

Jerroray emitted a round whistle of astonishment. " By George, that's so ! " she cried. " Your voice is just like Tom Nelson's ? That's what made me like you so much," she exclaimed, triumphantly. " I told you you reminded me of somebody nice, and it's that polite Mr. Nelson all the time."

" That's queer," said Tom. " What is there about my voice ? "

" It's sort of deep—and clear—and—and —gentlemanly," explained Jerroray.

" And you both pronounce your words different from us Westerners," said Jack Potts, in his hoarse, thick tones. " More like Easterners—but you're a Nebraskan, ain't you, too ? "

" Yes," said Tom.

" Native ? " queried Jack Potts, almost quizzically.

" Yes," said Tom.

" Well, now, he's answered one question, anyhow," exclaimed Miss Roray. " Maybe we can get his whole history if we keep on drawin' him out ten or a dozen years. Pretty slow fishin', though."

" Well," said Tom, somewhat embarrassed by the personal turn the talk had taken and the inconvenient definiteness of the fibs it had led him into. " I'm happy to resemble Mr. Tom Nelson in any particular. He's a plucky fellow, and has my sincere admiration."

" I like him, too," admitted Jack Potts. " If I run across him anywheres I'm not goin' to give him away. He stuck me for thirty dollars, but I charged it to the firm, and didn't bear him any malice, for he did it like a gentleman."

" Was you held up too ? " inquired Jerroray, eagerly. " Which time ? "

" First," replied Mr. Potts.

" Was you scared much ? "

" Well, no," and Mr. Potts smiled as if in pleasant reminiscence of his courage.

" Not ? What did you do then ? "

" Unfortunately I wasn't armed; but though I've carried a revolver ever since I've not had the luck to fall in with Mr. Nelson again—not when he was on the warpath, that is "—this with a quick look at Tom, intercepted by Miss Roray, who also glanced sharply, but with a puzzled expression at the innocent countenance of Mr. Chance, of Nebraska.

" But what would you do if you did fall in with him ? " she pursued, after a moment.

" I'd hold him up."

" How ? "

" That's a little private scheme of my own. I don't want to give it away and have some other feller get the glory of it. Besides, you might one of you go and tell Tom Nelson, and then he'd be on his guard," and Jack Potts gave Mr. Chance another suggestive look, which was again noticed by the young lady.

" You know it would really be an easy thing to hold him up," said Tom, oblivious to these signs.

" That's what I think," said Mr. Potts.

" Nerve and quickness, and your blinds closed so the men outside couldn't pop you off."

Jack Potts's face fell and he looked grave for a moment.

" I've made up my mind to keep my blinds down altogether on night trains now," went on Tom, "and to sit pretty well front in the car.   Then when Nelson is two-thirds of the way down just pop off the man at the top end and draw on him, and by that time there'd be half a dozen revolvers out."

" My ! " exclaimed Jerroray.   " Would you really dare ? "

" He might dare," said Mr. Potts, with sarcasm, " but doin' it's a different matter. Mr. Chance seems to have ideas on the subject, however," he went on.   " He's evidently been there."

" Been there ! " said Tom.   " I was never held up in my life."

" And never held anybody up either ? " queried Jack Potts, in the same half-jocose, half-suggestive manner as before.

" Held anybody up ? " said Tom, puzzled.   " Why, of course not.   But you know, I think it would be mighty good fun," he added.   " Miss Roray and I quite agree about it.   She wouldn't mind being an outlaw one bit, she says, so I'm going to try to persuade her to go on the road with me."

"You'd be a pretty successful team, I imagine," said Jack Potts, again in the suggestive tone, with a smile at Miss Roray.

That young woman, with a more than ever puzzled expression, started as if to blurt out some question, but Mr. Potts's finger on his lips stopped her with the words at the end of her tongue. Tom, sitting between the two, and with Jack Potts bending over him, did not notice this interchange of understanding, and Miss Roray quickly recovered herself.

"Chance hasn't ever asked me to drive double with him, yet," she said, with that frank and artless coquetry that Tom found so beguiling.

"Oh, I don't dare, of course — till I bring you the diamonds," he declared.

"What's that?" questioned Mr. Potts, with quick curiosity. Jerroray started to reply, but Tom stopped her.

"Don't tell him," he begged. "Don't tell anybody. I want the chance all to myself."

"But that ain't fair to me," said the young lady. "I want more Chances than one, you see."

" When that one is devoted to you, heart and soul ? " questioned Tom, impressively.

" Come, now—you're just gassing—you don't mean that," giggled the young lady.

" If there are any chances going, do give me one," put in Mr. Potts.

" Now I think that's only fair," said Jerroray. " I'll tell you, Potts, I've been engaged to Charley Shore, an Aurory feller, for two months, but it sort o' sickened me the way he behaved in the train robbery last night, so I says to Chance, says I, ' Charley'll get the mitten to-morrer,' says I. ' Poor Mr. Shore,' says he, ' but the world's the gainer '—meanin', as he explained, that it gave other fellers, includin' himself, a chance. So I says, says I, ' If it's chances you're talkin' about, the feller that brings me back my diamonds will have it all,' says I—and that's the chance Chance wants all to himself, but which, it seems to me, ain't fair to me. Now what do you think, Potts ? "

" I think Mr. Chance is awf'ly selfish, though I can't exactly blame him for it, for I'm sure in his place I'd have done the same thing. And I'd suggest, Miss Roray, that you don't tell any one else—leave it as a

duel, so to speak, between Chance and myself.''

'' Now you're as bad as he is.   I sha'n't
do that at all.   I shall tell everybody, even
poor little Charley Shore—and those what
wants the opportunity can take it.''

'' And I admire your spirit,'' bowed Jack
Potts, '' and I'm not sorry, after all, that
it's to be an open competition. And though
Mr. Chance may have means of securing
your jewels that are unknown to me, still I'll
wager even that I'm the man that does it.''

'' I take you,'' said Tom, '' and suggest
that Miss Roray hold the stakes, and buy
herself, in either event, a wedding-present
with them.''

Miss Roray promptly declared that she
gave no promises, and there mightn't be any
wedding—it was only a chance.   But the
young men protested themselves satisfied
with these terms, and the money agreed on
was accordingly placed in her hands.   In
the process of the transaction Tom emptied
his pockets, and his handkerchief, unnoticed
by him, fell to the floor and was picked up
by Mr. Potts.   An eager smile flitted across
that gentleman's countenance as he examined
the initials on it.

"Whose handkerchief is this?" he asked, in an indifferent tone. "Just picked it up here."

Tom felt in his empty pocket. "Must be mine," he said, reaching out his hand for it.

"They ain't your initials," said Mr. Potts, dryly.

Tom looked at them hastily. "So they aren't," he said, confused. "Some other fellow's lost it, after all."

"What are the initials?" asked Jerroray, noting the quiet smile on Jack Potts's face.

"T. N.," said that gentleman. "Do you know any such?"

"T. N.! Why," she cried, "those are Tom Nelson's initials!"

"Holy Moses!" ejaculated Mr. Potts. "You don't suppose he's anywheres on this train, do you? Darin' cuss if he is!"

The people immediately about them were taken into confidence, and then the matter was handed on to all the occupants of the car, but no one was found possessing the dangerous initials of "T. N." The fact that the handkerchief was discovered close by the seat occupied by Mr. Chance, of Nebraska, was often mentioned by Mr. Potts,

but quite carelessly, as if it had little significance. He also mentioned, with equal carelessness, that Mr. Chance had lost his handkerchief, but of course this wasn't his. Tom,
furious at his own heedlessness, appeared
confused and absent, a demeanor which was
suspicious both in the eyes of his enemies,
and in those of the friendly Jerroray, who
tried to divert him while the search was in
progress with her observations on men and
life. She looked at him with a renewed interest in her eyes, and did not pay much attention to Jack Potts when that young man
returned from his search.

"This handkerchief goes a-beggin'," he
said, "which ain't strange, considerin' that
the fellow who claims it lays himself open to
bein' hanged."

"You're funny," said Tom Norrie, contemptuously. "The idea of a train robber
having embroidered initials on his handkerchief, anyway. If Tom Nelson carries a
handkerchief at all it's most likely a red
bandanna."

"There are train robbers and train robbers," declared Jack Potts, sapiently.

"And drummers and drummers," retorted
Tom, with a sharp look at him.

9

Jack Potts met this home-thrust with so
quick a good-nature, and with so pleasant a
twinkle in his eyes, that in another moment
both young men laughed, and when Mr.
Potts held out his hand on the impulse of
the moment, Mr. Chance took it with no
lack of cordiality.

" There are plenty of people on this train,
however, who would be glad to view your
downfall, Mr. Chance," said the drummer,
" and for reasons that it does not take one
long to guess at"—here he smiled at Miss
Roray.   " I should advise you to be rather
circumspect as you walk the streets of Aurora, and give or take no cause of quarrel.
Or if you don't like that advice, at least have
your firearms handy."

" He's comin' up to see me," remarked
Jerroray, in a motherly manner.   " He'll
be safe up there.   I ain't anxious to quarrel
with him," and she bestowed upon Tom a
look of more than usual sweetness.

CHAPTER VIII

BLUFF

Innocence, though so greatly admired by the poets, and celebrated in many yards of verse, is at times highly dangerous to its possessor. Thus Tom Norrie, having a heart free of guile, and fearing no man, was not on the watch, and did not perceive more than half of what occurred on the train from Bud to Aurora. The curious fact that his voice resembled that of the outlaw, and that their methods of pronunciation were similar, had not entered his head as a cause of suspicion against him, for he had seen none of the suggestive glances exchanged by the drummer and Miss Roray apropos of this subject. The handkerchief incident had come near being unfortunate, and he cursed his own carelessness in not making way with such proof of his travelling under an assumed name. But, luckily, no one seemed to connect the handkerchief and its fatal

initials with him, and he had heard the
friendly Jack Potts state particularly to their
fellow-passengers, as he made his inquiries
of them, that it did not belong to Mr.
Chance.   He had not seen the slight smile
on the drummer's face, nor the glance of
meaning which had in some instances accompanied this statement, nor yet the return glance of understanding which had lit
the faces of certain gentlemen who already
stood towards him in the attitude of enemies.
So he felt that by denying his property before it was fastened on him irrevocably, he
had just managed to squeak out of a disagreeable contretemps, and he gave himself
no further uneasiness on the subject.   The
attention which his party attracted as they
alighted from the train, the degree to which
they seemed to be the object of many eyes,
if not of all, in the station, while he secured the luggage and Jack Potts talked
to Jerroray, he ascribed entirely to that
young lady's superlative good looks.   As
Mr. Neddy Bedloe had intimated in the
office of the Empire Hotel at Bud, she was
popular with her townsmen, and fame neces-
sarily attached to those who formed her
suite.

While Tom was awaiting his turn with the
baggage-man and reflecting thus agreeably
on the pleasure of paying court to a young
woman of the position and attractions of
his fair lady-friend, the lady-friend herself
was improving the opportunity to ask Mr.
Potts a few brief, but telling questions.

" Was that Chance's handkerchief? "

" It dropped out of his pocket."

" Did you actually see it drop out of his
pocket ? "

" I actually did."

" Why did you look for its initials before
giving it back to him ? "

" Pure curiosity," and Jack Potts smiled
genially.

" You don't think it's possible that he
is "—she stopped, interrupted by the look
of alarm on the drummer's face.

" My dear young lady, don't you suggest
such a thing," he said, quickly.   " It's as
much as the man's life is worth !   Here are
all these Aurora gentlemen ready to cut his
throat for the favor you've shown him.   It
would take only those two words that you
just didn't say to cause them to produce the
sheriff and the whole police force and clap
Mr. Chance into jail on the mere suspicion.

If you take any interest in that young man you'd better be pretty careful."

" I take an interest in Tom Nelson," declared Miss Roray.

" Happy man, if only he knew it," murmured Mr. Potts. " *I* shall never tell him."

" Say," inquired Miss Roray, suddenly, " what's the matter with your voice ? It changes. Most of the time it sounds sort of hoarse, as if you had a cold or somethin'. But just then, when you said ' happy man,' and before, when you said ' my dear young lady,' it sounded as smooth as—as———"

" As a good cocktail," suggested Jack Potts, with a smile. " It's emotion does it, Miss Roray—pure emotion. Love changes a man from a roarin' lion to a suckin' dove —so why shouldn't it alter his voice from a roar to a coo ? "

Jerroray tossed her head consciously. " Cuckoo I guess," she remarked. " And a lot of love there is about it."

" Now let me tell you somethin'," said Jack Potts, seriously. " Love is catchin'. When a man sees half a dozen other men in love with the same girl it makes him think she must be a pretty nice girl. And if he's the kind of man that likes to get what other people want, and leave them whistlin', why it's all the more so. Under such conditions, love practically at first sight ain't a bit impossible. I won't say more—for various reasons besides the fact that our friend Mr. Chance is approachin' us—but in case we shouldn't meet again right away I would like to ask you not to forget me, even if you don't see your diamonds so soon as you've a right to expect." The bold, handsome face of Mr. Potts was softened to so genuine a tenderness, and he spoke these last words so impressively, that Miss Roray was thrilled in spite of herself as she met his eyes, and did not resist him when he took her hand for a moment, with a warmer pressure than the length of their acquaintance might seem to justify. The hand pressure gave her another thrill, and thus there was a vivid color in her cheeks, and she looked handsomer than ever, as she turned to meet Mr. Chance, of Nebraska, arriving with her bag in one hand and his own in the other. Tom saw these signs of the times, and laughed to think what a flirt she was. It not only relieved him from any sense of responsibility about the vigorous flirtation he was himself carrying

on with her, but lent indeed an added zest
to that encounter.

The Roray equipage, a dusty buggy drawn
by a sorrel pacing mare, was in waiting
without the station, in charge of what looked
to Tom like a middle - aged cowboy, who
might have seen better days—that is, his costume could hardly have been worse. He sat
in a dégagé attitude, with one foot on the
dashboard and the other dangling outside,
peacefully masticating the customary quid.
Jerroray said " Hullo, Ernest," to him, and
he replied " Hullo, Jerry," to her without
in the least deranging himself, or offering to
assist her in. The two young men were only
too ready to perform this service for her,
and when it was accomplished she refused
any further attendance.

" It's dinner-time, and you'd only be in
the way," she explained, pleasantly. " Terence would think I was crazy if I turned up
with two strange gents in tow. I'll go
ahead and explain things to him and then
you can come along up in the afternoon.
Say, we'll have afternoon tea ! Dad brought
me the whole outfit last time he went to
Bloomer, and I've never used it yet. Come
early and stay late," she called out as the

man drove her off. Before they turned the corner she had taken the reins in her own hands and was conversing affably with her stolid attendant.

"A most extraordinary young woman," observed Tom to Jack Potts, quite as if that gentleman shared his own point of view in regard to the peculiarities of the West. He perceived this incongruity himself before Mr. Potts had time to reply, and turned and looked at him quickly, wondering what he would say.

Jack Potts was smiling, as in fact he had been doing most of the time since he met him, thought Tom. "I suppose they don't grow like that in Nebraska?" he inquired.

"We have them of all kinds in Nebraska," returned Tom with as much nonchalance as he could muster, "but Jerroray strikes me as an original, viewed in the light of any civilization—even Nebraskan. At all events, she's the best-looking girl I've come across, and her manners strike me as equally unique and pleasing."

"I'm a good deal taken with her myself," observed the drummer. "But it looks as if Tom Nelson had got the refusal of that particular peach."

" Not if some other gentleman matches Mr. Nelson's valor—it's what he does she likes—not himself."

" Now, look here, Chance, do you really think you or any other feller could get those diamonds away from Nelson ? " inquired Jack Potts.

" I don't know," replied Tom, with candor, " but it wouldn't be bad fun to try, for if there's a man I should like to meet it's that one."

" Well, now, why, I'd like to know ? "

" Because he strikes me as uncommonly clever and uncommonly interesting—a man, as one might say, out of ten thousand."

" And you ain't afraid of him ? " queried Jack Potts, with his customary quizzical smile.

" No," said Tom. " I ain't, although you seem to think that's mere talk. But my idea of Tom Nelson is that he's a good fellow. It seems odd, perhaps, to regard a highway robber in that light, but all that I hear of him confirms me in it. In short, I can't help feeling that to me just at present a week with Tom Nelson would be worth a cycle of Cathay."

" A Nebraskan who quotes Tennyson," observed Mr. Potts, derisively.

"And a Chicago drummer who recognizes it," retorted Tom Norrie.

"Well," said Mr. Potts, "though I've fallen somewhat from my high estate, I don't mind admitting that I was once at Harvard College."

"So was I," admitted Tom, with a grin.

"All the way from Nebraska?"

"All the way from Nebraska," said Tom, unblushingly. "What was your class?"

"We shall have to defer our college reminiscences, I fear," said Mr. Potts, with a smile, "for here we are at the Palace Hotel. But your being a Harvard man was no news to me," he added, as they walked into the hotel office and bar-room.

"What do you mean? How did you know it?" inquired Tom, with quick curiosity.

But Jack Potts was already engaged in conversation with the hotel clerk and proprietor in one, who seemed, like Mr. Dicker, to be an old friend of his, and Tom received no answer to his question. After a few moments he introduced Tom to this gentleman, whom Tom had been regarding with interest as representing Mr. Dicker's idea of a chump. He was a short, stout young man,

with a large, round, clean-looking face which
was embellished with two very red lips,
two very pink cheeks, a small curling blond
mustache and a dimpled chin. This bright-
colored countenance was saved from mere
pink-and-white effeminacy by a pair of
small but unusually sharp blue eyes, which
had the appearance of taking in everything
at a glance. Thus while Tom was taking
him in and regarding the careless grace of
the undeniably négligé costume which had
called forth the scorn of the elegant Mr.
Dicker, he too was not idle, and Tom imagined that he could have given a complete
inventory of his own attire and visible belongings after the two or three good-humored
but keen glances that he had flashed toward
our hero. His name was Keach—J. Cutler
Keach—and he appeared to possess those
qualities of popularity which were wanting
in the self-centred Mr. Dicker. He assigned
rooms to Mr. Chance and Mr. Potts and
went himself to show them the way, but
with true appreciation of his own dignity
allowed Tom to carry his grip unchallenged
—Mr. Potts being burdened only with a
light bag slung over his shoulder. They
were met in the hall by a fifteen-year-old

fac-simile of Mr. Keach, who began ringing an enormous gong, much to the distress of their ears. Tom laughed at the ludicrous resemblance of the two, and though he formed the tail of the procession this mirth did not escape the eagle eye of his host.

" Younger brother," he observed, laconically on the stairs, in a glad interval of the gong-ringing.

" T. Corson Keach," supplemented Jack Potts for Tom's further information.

Tom gazed with delight upon the spotlessness of his small apartment and of everything in it, then opened the tough-looking extension bag for which he had traded his own neat Gladstone in Kansas City, and secured for himself a fresh handkerchief to replace the one now in the possession of Mr. Potts. Before he put it in his pocket, however, he cut off, with a diagonal slash of his penknife, the whole corner where the telltale initials were embroidered, rolled this rag up, tossed it out of the window into the gutter, and rejoined his friend, whom he heard whistling in the corridor without.

On entering the dining-room shortly afterwards, Tom laughed aloud at the sight of the waiter girls who were nimbly ministering

to the needs of some thirty men or so and
half a dozen women, all eating for dear life.
They were very stout, but very agile, and
they looked exactly like each other, and exactly like J. Cutler and T. Corson Keach.

Jack Potts smiled.   " M. Jane Keach and
S. Maria Keach," he explained, in an undertone, after they had sat down.   " A. Ma-
tilda Keach does the cookin', G. Washington Keach, aged ten or so, runs errands,
and A. Lincoln Keach is boss in the liv-
ery stable.   They're one of the features
of Aurora, and even the inhabitants can't
hardly tell 'em apart.   They keep the clean-
est hotel I ever struck in one of these half-
baked little Western cities, and that's very
much to their credit.   J. Cutler is a first-
rate feller, but, like many otherwise sensible men, he has one fatal fad—he thinks
he's gifted as a detective.   Thus he regards
all guests in the house in the light of possible fugitives from crime, which at times is
a little embarrassin' to the guests.   He'll
prob'ly ask you questions in an artfully artless manner peculiar to himself, but I don't
feel afraid he'll get much out of you."

The etiquette of the dinner-table at the
Palace Hotel of Aurora seemed to be to eat

as much as you can in the least possible
time, say nothing during the process, and
then get out the instant you have taken your
last mouthful, but before you have finished
its mastication ; that is, if you masticate at
all, as many prefer not to do. The men
finished and bolted one by one, almost without a word—though not without toothpicks.
It seemed impossible to break so preternat-
ural a hush, upon which one's remarks must
needs be painfully audible to the entire as-
semblage, so Tom held his peace, took what
was set before him, and contented himself
with observing the society in which he found
himself.   Miners and ranchmen were the
chief ingredients, with a sprinkling of more
or less dapper gentlemen, who, according to
Tom's experience, might be real estate and
insurance men, grocery clerks, and druggists,
or even lawyers and doctors.   Some had
their " ladies " with them—faded looking
women with painted cheeks—and there were
a few unwholesome infants, whose table
manners were even more atrocious than those
of his small cousins, thought Tom.   He had
seen of late many such dismal hotel dining-
rooms, and found nothing new in this one,
except the fat-faced waiting maids, whose

active movements and glib speech he followed with fascinated eyes and ears. Jack Potts was evidently a favorite with them, and they bestowed upon him many nods and becks and wreathed smiles as they passed and repassed, waiting on him and his neighbors. This by no means surprised Tom, for he found the drummer remarkably attractive himself, and had noted, too, the immediate effect which he produced on the blooming Jerroray. There was a coolness about him, a dash and a go, which, joined to his good looks and vigor, made one think that he must be interesting. Tom wondered how much of his attractiveness lay in surface charms, and how much of it in the man's real essence.

"A drummer—and, above all, a drummer in the jewelry trade," he said to himself—"is hardly what we are apt to think of as a large man, or even an interesting one, yet he gives me the idea of force, and I find myself instinctively wishing all the time to know more about him. Now there couldn't be much more to know about a jewelry drummer. And besides, he's been at Harvard, and I don't believe men are generally fitted for the jewelry trade by courses at Harvard College."

The room was now nearly empty, and they were consuming their pie—of which they had had a magnificent choice of about a dozen sorts—when just at this point of Tom's thoughts Jack Potts turned to him with his usual smiling expression.

" I wonder if you happen to be wantin' anything in the jewelry line ? " he inquired. " I'd be glad to show you my samples," and he tapped lightly the bag slung at his side.

Tom gazed at him very seriously. " How long have you been in the jewelry trade ? " he asked.

" That's rather a leadin' question," laughed Mr. Potts, " but I don't know as I mind tellin' you that I've been there— well—quite as long, I'll wager, as you've lived in Nebraska."

Tom could not avoid smiling at this unexpected rejoinder. " You don't at all give one the impression of a man who has spent his life in trade," he retorted. " Evidently you're not naturally a business man, or, after so long an apprenticeship, you wouldn't still be a drummer."

" I'm really head of the firm," said Jack Potts, assuming a confidential tone, " but

10

I go out on the road occasionally as a sort of a vacation from the cares of business. Drummin's first rate fun, in my opinion.''

'' Mr. Moses, then, I suppose? or possibly Finkstein?''

Jack Potts, rising to leave the dining-room, answered this question only with a smile at first, but as they passed through the hall on the way to the bar-room he remarked, blandly: '' I'd no more think of travellin' under an alias than you would.''

A loud roar of conversation came through the closed door of the bar-room, but it ceased instantly when the door opened and Mr. Potts and Mr. Chance entered that sanctum of conviviality. Every eye was turned upon them, except the left orb of a cross-eyed ranchman who stood within five feet, and Tom observed that he shifted his organs of vision about once in thirty seconds, as if to give each eye a chance. This performance had much the air of turning search-lights off and on, and our hero's risibilities were so actively excited thereby that he could hardly help laughing in the gentleman's face. But he began to feel curiously that he was himself the object of prominence, that the eyes were fixed rather on him than on Jack Potts,

and that it would be well to be discreet in
his behavior.   He recalled the drummer's
advice on the train, and wondered, in a somewhat puzzled way, if paying attentions to
Jerroray was really going to be so serious as
all that.   Then, beside the bar, he caught
sight of Charley Shore's discontented, pretty-
face, close up to the round visage of Mr. J.
Cutler Keach, and perceived, from the direction of their eyes, that they were discussing
him.   He felt that he must act at once, with
resolution and promptness, and without be-
traying that he realized himself to be the object of enmity.

"Would there be any harm in setting up
drinks all around?" he asked of Mr. Potts,
in an undertone.

"No, indeed.   Great idea," answered
that gentleman.

So Tom, with composure, made a little
speech of those few well-chosen words that
are always used by amateur orators.   He said
in substance that he had been but a short
time in Aurora, but that he was greatly
taken with the town and its attractions, in-
cluding the hotel, which was a tidy credit
to the family of Keach, etc., etc., and that,
in short, he should like to invite all the

gentlemen present to join with him in drinking the health of their charming little city.

This was immediately done with a great good will, and Tom felt afterwards that though they still looked at him as if he were an escaped curiosity, there was certainly a benevolence in their scrutiny that had not been there before. The frown on Mr. Shore's countenance convinced him further that he had done wisely and well. He started to take out his handkerchief at this point, forgetting in his complaisance that he had resolved to use it only in discreet privacy, but a touch on his elbow stopped him half way.

"I should think you'd had enough difficulty with handkerchiefs for one day," said Jack Potts in an undertone, and then laughed as if he had been telling a good story. Tom look bewildered. " Laugh you d—n fool," said Jack Potts, forcibly. "And wipe your mouth on your sleeve like your betters." Tom laughed then as if the joke were a capital one, and Mr. Potts joined with him in an innocent and hearty manner that caused Tom to envy him his powers of dissimulation. Jack Potts whispered one more

word in his ear as if it were an addendum to
the joke.   " Get out of this as soon as you
can.   It ain't the safest place in the world
just at present.   And don't loaf round town
much."   Whereupon they both laughed
again.

Then Jack Potts moved up to Mr. Shore
and Mr. Keach, and began talking to them
in the same undertone, as if he were telling
them the same joke.

" By George ! " exclaimed Charley Shore,
" that's a good one."

Tom observed that Mr. Keach still had his
eye on him, however, and bought a few
cigars as he paid his score, hoping to propi-
tiate him thereby and then get away.

" Terrible train robberies," observed Mr.
Keach, carelessly.

" Yes, awful," answered Tom.

" Guess there'll be no more, though,"
this with a watchful glance.

" Why so ? "

" Got our eye on the thief."

" You've not caught him, have you ? "

" No, but we will."

" That's interesting.   I'd like to be present."

" Could be managed easily."

" Well, let me know beforehand.   I shall
be round here a few days.   I'm rather interested in the man."

" Smart old cuss," said J. Cutler Keach,
as if he were thinking of something else.

" Old ? " said Tom, in surprise.

" Sixty, if he's a day," rejoined Mr.
Keach.

" Are you sure of it ? "

" Sure as we want to be."

" Well, I hope you'll catch him then,"
said Tom, with a laugh.   " An old villain
always seems so much worse than a young
one."   This was a new and interesting
view of Mr. Nelson, and he was anxious
to discuss the matter further with J. Cutler
Keach, but remembering Jack Potts's warning he took out his watch.   " I'll have to
go out now on my business," he observed,
" but I'll be back again by and by, and
should be glad to continue this conversation.
Young or old, Mr. Nelson is certainly an
interesting gentleman, if one may judge by
the number of different opinions about him,
and I should like to hear yours, as I understand you're clever at detective work."

" Who—me ?   Reckon somebody's been
stuffin' you," said Mr. Keach—this modest

disclaimer accompanied by a pleased smile. "But you're welcome to my opinion if you'll give me yours."

"It's a bargain," said Tom. He lighted one of his cigars, looked about the room where the company in little knots was now engaged in low conversation, observed that Jack Potts was still holding Mr. Shore with his glittering tongue, and then proceeded to get himself out by the street door with as much coolness and nonchalance as he could summon. As he walked across the room the same complete silence as before fell upon it. Every one was looking at him, but he pretended not to notice. J. Cutler Keach whispered a word in the ear of one of the later editions of his name, who deftly wound his way through the crowd in our hero's wake. Tom passed through the screen doors, which flapped together behind him, and down the steps into the street. Instantly he heard in the room he had left an uproar of excited talk, which stirred his blood and made his heart beat. What did it mean? What was going to happen? Was he about to be lynched for his attentions to the belle of Aurora? Or did they connect him in some curious way with the outlaw, Tom Nelson? No, that was too crazy and impossible—it must be merely that they were all devoted to Jerroray and incensed that he should seem to cut them out.

" Well, they shan't scare me off," he said to himself, with grim determination on his face. He purchased in the first shop he came to half a dozen high-colored handkerchiefs that seemed to him more suited to the climate than his own ; and then secured a man to drive him to the residence of the Sheriff—which proved to be a showy mansion on a slight eminence, three-quarters of a mile from the centre of the town.

CHAPTER IX

" He's the man," declared J. Cutler Keach with conviction the instant Tom had disappeared, and on this statement being questioned vociferously, he narrated with considerable embellishment the conversation which had just taken place between him and the bogus Mr. Chance. " He's a plucky gent to come here and defy us in our midst, but he ain't overburdened with intellect or he'd have been sharp enough not to let on how surprised he was when I said Tom Nelson was old. ' Hope you'll catch him, then,' said he, smilin' away to himself. ' An' I'll come back to-night and talk it over with you.' Thinks he'll throw sand in my eyes, does he? Guess I ain't waitin' till he comes back to-night ! ''

" Where's the initials you found ?" asked Jack Potts.

Mr. Keach proudly displayed the dusty, three-cornered rag of Tom's handkerchief.

" How do you know that's his ? Did you see him drop it ? "

" George Washington was comin' home from school an' seen it thrown out the window of No. 13, and run and picked it up."

" With true Keach curiosity," put in Jack Potts, smilingly.

" We Keaches is born with the idea that things don't happen without reason," said J. Cutler, with genial pride. " So George Washington brings it to me and asks me if I know any ' T. N.'—which I don't, but I'd like to, says I to G. W. An' then I remember what you remarked about Mr. Chance, an' then in a minute in comes Charley Shore an' tells me all he knows."

" Which don't take long," said a voice from the crowd.

" An' then some other gentlemen with ideas on the subject, an' we puts two an' two together——"

" And find you have eight or ten," laughed Mr. Potts.

" Well, what we've got is enough to arrest him on, anyhow," returned J. Cutler Keach.

" An' he'll be languishin' in jail in about one hour," stated Mr. Charley Shore, triumphantly.

Jack Potts started. "Have you got out a warrant?" he asked, quickly.

"No," answered Mr. Shore; "but that don't take long. An' the Terror's right handy at the Court House to-day. I just seen him comin' back from dinner."

At this moment the youthful Keach returned, breathless. "Bought—himself—some — pocky hankershers — at Joe Pye's notion store," he declared, in jerks, while the crowd exchanged glances of excited conviction, "then — then—got the Blubber — to drive him — up to the Terror's house!"

Everybody looked very much surprised and half incredulous at this statement, except Charley Shore and the perennially smiling Mr. Potts.

"Great Scott, he's got the nerve!"

"Don't mind puttin' his head in the lion's mouth!"

"Now, you know a man can't help admirin' such a cool cuss as that——"

Charley Shore sniffed impatiently at these comments. "He's after the girl — that don't take no nerve—an' the Sheriff's a mile away down town here."

"Do you mean Miss Jerroray?" in-

quired Mr. Keach. " Never heard you re-
fer to her as ' the girl' before."

" ' The gurrl' give him the mitten since
Tom Nelson held him up last night—that's
why.   An' Charley ain't over fond of either
her or Tom Nelson to-day."   This was Mr.
Neddy Bedloe's contribution to the discussion, and as it produced an immediate effect,
he proceeded to take advantage of the pleasing prominence it brought him into by nar-
rating briefly the occurrences of the night
before at Bud's great ball, while the crowd
listened eagerly.

" Well, he's got good taste in gals," com-
mented one man.

" They ain't many fellers as would be a
match for Jerroray—but I reckon Tom Nelson would," said another.

" Seems a pity to disturb their taty-tate,"
observed a third.   " I vote we gives 'em a
couple hours or so for spoonin', 'fore we go
up after him."

These remarks incensed Mr. Shore beyond
endurance.   " You think it's nice for the
Honorable Terence Roray's daughter to be
spoonin' with a train-robber — a common
thief, do you ?   You think that would be a
nice match to encourage ?   All of you're

afraid of him ; though there are thirty of you, you don't dare go up an' face him all by himself ! ''

" Nor yet all by Jerroray,'' put in Mr. Potts, with a sympathetic gravity that brought down the house.

" Say, Charley, if you've got all that agin him why don't you call him out ? '' queried a good - looking young fellow in full new cowboy rig.

" Seems to me you'd orter settle the private quarrel before the law puts its finger in the pie—you won't get no chance afterwards,'' said an older man.

" Mr. Shore ain't over handy with his revolver, an' he ain't goin' to take no risks if he can get other folks to take 'em for him,'' remarked one of the dapper and clerk-like boarders with a facetious wink to everybody within range of his eye.

" You shut up, Andy Slade, or you'll take bigger risks than you'll like,'' said Mr. Shore, angrily.

The crowd immediately cleared around them, while Messrs. Shore and Slade looked daggers and six-shooters and Winchester rifles at each other ; but whether either of them would have proceeded from these kill-

ing looks to murderous actions will never be
known, for Mr. J. Cutler Keach, weary of
so much talk, burst in at this point with for-
cible recommendations to the crowd at large
that they should sink private animosities for
the public good and proceed to business.
He stated the case of the State against Tom
Nelson with eloquent brevity, reminded them
that Mr. Nelson was now within their reach,
but was not likely to be so long, that it
would redound eternally to their credit if
they caught him, and eternally to their dis-
credit if they lost him, and that here was
Aurora's great chance to show that she
needed neither Pinkertons nor Byrneses from
outside, as had been insultingly suggested
by rival cities not five hundred miles away,
but that she was amply able to work out her
own salvation from within, with her own
superior resources of intellect and detective
ability. Mr. Keach wound up with the
practical suggestion that they should repair
at once to No. 13, the chamber assigned Mr.
Chance, of Nebraska, and explore the pos-
sessions of that very suspicious character,
with an eye to the discovery of more T. N.'s.

The crowd, with the strange human and
sheeplike instinct to follow anyone who has

force enough to want to lead, was strongly
swayed by the vigor of Mr. Keach's mind,
and for the moment his wishes were its own.
In thirty seconds they would have had in
their hands all the incriminating T. N.'s of
Tom Norrie's neatly marked linen, and
would have been hot on his trail, but just
here Mr. Potts interposed with the suggestion that they should pause and reflect.   To
break into Mr. Chance's room and investigate his belongings without authority, which,
in case they were mistaken, would put them
in a humiliating and ridiculous position, and
perhaps even a dangerous one, if Mr. Chance
himself should turn up inopportunely, was
possibly not the best way of securing their
ends.   A warrant for his arrest would be a
safer means at least, was easily secured if
there was any one willing to swear it out,
and would enable them to investigate Mr.
Chance and his property at their leisure and
under the protection of the law.

Even with his manner of cool indifference,
his ironical, half-humorous way of speaking,
there was apparently as much power to move
men in Jack Potts as in the estimable Mr.
Cutler Keach.   The drummer, while ap-
pearing to side entirely with Mr. Keach in

his condemnation of Tom Nelson's awful
crimes, and his desire to bring the villain to
justice, somehow brought out almost immediately in the crowd the sentiment of sympathy with the outlaw and of admiration for
his bold deeds which to Tom Norrie had
been so striking a thing in the talk he heard
of him at the Empire Hotel at Bud. The
men were by no means sure, after all, that
they wouldn't like to see so smart a cuss as
he, and one so d——d plucky, get away
with flying colors and leave justice to
whistle. Mr. Keach was in despair, and so,
to all outward seeming, was Mr. Potts, who
stood by Mr. Keach as his most sympathetic
ally, yet all the time by little artful remarks
and insinuations of the greatest apparent
simplicity fanned that temper in the crowd
which he represented himself as most desir-
ous to allay.

The drummer also encouraged a wordy al-
tercation that arose as to who should swear
out the warrant. Everybody except Mr.
Shore thought Mr. Shore the man to do it,
but he insisted that it should be Mr. Keach.
Mr. Keach said he'd just as lief do it, but
he wasn't goin' to be bossed by nobody, and
he hadn't been to Bud, and Charley Shore

had, and it was much more 'propriate that
Charley Shore should do it, and if he wasn't
willin' to he'd just better give the whole
thing up.

Mr. Shore finally accepted this view of
the situation, but he needed even then so
much bolstering before he could be brought
to the point of action, that it was more than
an hour before the first practical steps were
taken, and a full hour and a half before the
necessary warrant was sworn out for the arrest of Tom Nelson, train robber, travelling
under the alias of J. Chance, of Nebraska.

And long before this dénouement was
reached Jack Potts had withdrawn himself
reluctantly from the counsels of Mr. Keach,
on the plea of the absolute necessity that
he should finish up his business at Aurora
and reach Bloomer that night.   He walked
rapidly down the main street of the town,
and went into a corner sample-room, three
blocks from the hotel.   He left this establishment two minutes later, by the side-door,
and turned soon from the side street in
which he found himself into a narrow, strag-
gling alley.   In a moment he was out of
sight of the street he had just left, and alone
also in the alley.   He started into a rapid

11

fox-trot, keeping a constant lookout behind him as he ran ; but no one appeared, and he soon arrived at a door on which he gave three quick knocks, followed in an instant by another three. The door was at once unbolted, and he was inside what appeared to be the joint residence of a man and a horse, both of whom showed great delight at the sight of him.

" Saddle Folly as quick as you can," said Jack Potts, and as the man flew about his task he himself put on the bridle, kissing the mare's soft nose as he did so. " Have you had her out to-day ? " he asked.

" No, sorr.   She come in last night so wet that I thinks to meself she won't need more'n three miles the day, an' I'll give her that at evenin', I will, when there ain't no one a-lookin'."

" That's all right, Mick.   She'll get a good pull now, the beauty," and Jack Potts vaulted into his saddle from the ground, like a boy full of surplus energy.

" She'll be good fer it, too," said the Irishman, opening the door to let them pass out.   " She warn't no more blowed last night than if she'd been out for just a can-ter."

Horse and rider sped away on an easy lope
out of the town, and then skirted it in a
rapid circuit, which brought them soon into
the rear of Mr. Terence Roray's big white
residence, sitting on its little hill. Ernest
came out the back door as they rode up, and
Jack Potts looked at him sharply before dis-
mounting.

" I've got five gold eagles in my pocket for
you if you can keep your mouth shut," he
said, almost sternly. " And there's no time
to lose. Will you do it ? "

" Reckon I will," said Ernest, meeting
the look squarely.

" You'll do," said Potts briefly, satisfied
with his scrutiny. " Keep the women folks
quiet, too, and let the other feller that'll
come out here in one minute or less take this
mare and go where he d—n pleases. The
sheriff's down town, isn't he ? "

" Yes," replied the laconic Ernest.

Jack Potts entered the back door as famil-
iarly as if he had been there before, but the
big, good-natured looking Irish woman in
the kitchen gave a faint scream and threw
up her hands at her first look at him.

" Great luck ! " cried Jack Potts. " It's
Micky's wife ! You can do me a fine turn,

Biddy, and put money in your pocket and Mick's.   There's a young man in with Miss Roray that has got to get out of town mighty quick or he'll be arrested in about five minutes and get into the lockup.   I want to see him this instant, and I'll give you your directions later, but if the crowd should turn up before I expect, just remember one thing, the black mare ain't mine, she's Mr. Chance's, and he got away on her before I could nab him.   Do you catch on?''

Biddy looked perfect intelligence.   '' Yis, I catches on, Mr.——,'' and she hesitated, with a twinkle in her eyes.

'' Potts,'' supplied the drummer.   '' Jack Potts.   Now for Miss Roray.''

Biddy led him at once to the parlor. '' Here's a gintleman wants to see you sure, Jerry,'' she explained, as she stood wiping her hands on her apron, in the door of the gilded and frescoed apartment, gorgeous. with shaded plush furniture of four different colors.

Jerroray rose, startled, from her tea-table, which was of uncommon size, and set as if for a meal, with coarse plates and knives and forks in high contrast to the dainty tea-cups from Bloomer.   The idea of a tea-gown in the mind of Aurora's belle seemed to be a mixture of a ball dress and a Mother Hubbard wrapper, for she was at once décolletée and minus a waist line. But the bizarre costume was brilliantly becoming, and her complexion was unimpaired by the garish daylight. Both she and Mr. Chance looked flushed and happy, and it required no discernment to scent flirtation in the very air.

A pained expression came on the face of Mr. Potts, but he bore up heroically and proceeded at once to business, wasting no time on preliminaries. With a mere statement of the situation he urged Mr. Chance to fly immediately. " You're not safe in this town an instant. They've raided your room, and are as sure you're Tom Nelson as—as I'm sure you're not! Take the horse waitin' at the back-door, ride down the hill and straight· toward the sun for three miles as near as you can judge. Then give the mare her head, let her take her own gait—it's a fast one—and she'll bring you to a safe place before night. The people'll take care of you and no questions asked, and you're to stay quiet till you hear from me. I'll give you a good long start, and then if Miss Roray will lend me one of her father's horses——"

"I'll lend you my own horse," said Jerroray, with pride.

"I'll make a feint of chasin' you, just to put the people off the track. It would be as much as my head's worth if they knew I'd helped you off."

"By George, Potts, you're a good fellow," said Tom, warmly, seizing his hand. "You've saved my life."

"No—Folly'll do that. She ain't a horse I'm in the habit of lendin' even to my best friends, but she's the only person that can get you out of this scrape. Now, away with you. Miss Roray can see you off if she likes, but I'll stay here so's not to give the man outside there any more lies to tell than are absolutely necessary. Put all your trust in Folly—she'll beat wisdom out of his boots any day in the week."

Tom stayed for no more, but with a warm pressure of Miss Roray's hand at the kitchen door, and one look into her fine eyes, responsive now with the excitement, he leaped to the saddle and was off down the hill and straight into the west on a freed hand-gallop.

Jerroray stood on the back steps shading her eyes with her hand, her face flushed and her lips parted, while Ernest leaned against the house, both staring after the rapidly diminishing horse and rider.

"My, but ain't that a pretty horse!" said the young lady.

"I never see a neater, and not a spot on her nowheres," declared Ernest. "You bet your little life she can go some."

Here Biddy touched the rapt Jerroray on her shoulder. "The gintleman inside would like to spake to ye, Jerry," she said, with a broad Irish grin on her good Irish face.

Mr. Potts had come out into the kitchen to view the departure, and now communicated to Miss Roray his wishes as to what story should be told by herself, Ernest, and Biddy. "Biddy here's all right," he said, while the increased breadth of Biddy's grin corroborated him, "and I fixed the man with a sum of money, but if he understands he's servin' your interests as well——"

"Exactly," said Jerroray. "I see, an' he'll do it, too." She started promptly to go out the door again.

"Wait," said Mr. Potts, taking out his watch. "I'll follow our friend in about ten minutes if Ernest will have the horse ready, and meanwhile he'd better keep a sharp lookout towards the town and let us know the moment he sees any one comin'.''

It did not take Miss Roray long to communicate the drummer's wishes, strongly emphasized by her own, to the slouchy Ernest, and she reappeared in the kitchen with a rapidity which indicated that ten minutes was none too long for all she had to say to Mr. Potts.

'' Come on into the parlor,'' she said, leading the way. '' I was forgettin' you'd got to be off after him so quick. I'll give you some afternoon tea.''

'' Suppose I prefer morning tea—tea of the dawn—Aurora tea ? '' he inquired, as she poured out a mixture suspiciously dark-colored.

'' Say, we ain't got time to joke. I want you to explain.''

'' Explain what ? ''

'' Everything. He is Tom Nelson, ain't he ? ''

'' There's no proof, but your friend Mr. Shore and Mr. J. Cutler Keach are sure of it.''

'' Is Charley Shore at the bottom of this ? '' inquired the young lady with flashing eyes.

'' Mr. Shore is certainly very much interested in securing Mr. Chance's arrest," said the drummer.

"I'll pay him back well," declared Jerroray, with a most vicious and revengeful expression. "What business has he got, I'd like to know, to interfere with—with——" she stopped self-consciously.

"With your love affairs?" suggested Jack Potts. "Is it a love affair—so soon?" he asked, with a touch of real earnestness in his voice, as he leaned forward in his chair to get a better view of her face.

"No," she replied, with prompt but somehow unconvincing disclaimer; then added, in a moment, "but I told you I was in love with Tom Nelson."

Mr. Potts set down his cup of tea with a grave face. "I've half a mind to tell you somethin'," he said, thoughtfully. "They say women can't keep secrets, but you strike me as a woman that could if she wanted to."

"You needn't tell me any secrets if you're afraid I'll give 'em away," said Jerroray, proudly, "but I never went back on anybody yet."

"I can well believe that," said Jack Potts. "You strike me as an uncommonly good feller in every way. By the by, do you ride?'' he asked, irrelevantly.

'' I should smile !'' asseverated the young lady. ''You can judge by my horse, the Red Devil, that you're agoin' to take. I trained him myself, after two men had given him up. He's a bute, too, though maybe he ain't so fast as your mare. But he's thoroughbred, every inch of him, like she is, too, I suppose?''

'' Yes, Folly's certainly thoroughbred,'' said Mr. Potts, absently, with his eyes fixed on his companion's face.

'' I don't see how if you're a drummer you happen to have a horse lyin' round loose so handy in Aurory,'' went on Jerroray, with sudden suspicion. '' And besides this ain't tellin' me your secret—even if I am a good feller.''

'' It ain't exactly a secret,'' said Mr. Potts. '' It's only a fact. Only I don't want you to tell anyone that I told it to you. It's merely that though our lately departed friend ain't Mr. Chance, he ain't Tom Nelson either.''

'' Do you know that?''

''I do.''

'' Could you prove it?''

"I could."

"Well, why didn't you, then, and keep that jealous little chump, Charley Shore, from actin' up so and drivin' him out of town?"

"Well, now, that *is* a secret, Miss Roray. No, don't look like that; it's a secret you'll know all about some day, if you'll let me tell it to you, but it's a long story, and there isn't time now. I had good reasons for not provin' that Mr. Chance wasn't Tom Nelson, and you see he hasn't suffered. He'll have a lot of fun out of it, too, and perhaps he'll meet the great Tom Nelson before he's through with his adventures, and that'll make him happy."

"Then he'll get me my diamonds back!"

"He's not very likely to do that," said Mr. Potts, with a smile. "Don't expect impossibilities of an Eastern tenderfoot."

"Eastern tenderfoot!" exclaimed Miss Roray.

"You surely didn't think he came from Nebraska, did you?" inquired Mr. Potts. "He's an Easterner and a Harvard man, out here on a lark, and under an assumed name, so that if he gets into difficulties his family won't know it. He's a first-rate feller, too, and I like him, or I wouldn't have taken all

this trouble to save his precious hide, and
lent him the best mare he ever threw a leg
over.   But he won't bring you back your
diamonds—mark my words ! ''

" Will you, then? ''

" My dear young lady, Tom Nelson's a
man of gallantry, who don't suffer other
gentlemen to do his duty for him.   If you
receive your diamonds back it'll be from
his own hands.   I can't even hope that he'll
let me be his emissary.   He's seen you, and
that's enough.   They've told me what he
said to you on the train, and he'll keep that
half promise as religiously as if he'd taken
his oath.''

" My, but he must be a dandy! '' cried
Jerroray, enthusiastically.   " An' you seem
to know a lot about him ? ''

" I've met him, as I told you,'' said Mr.
Potts.   " But what's more to the point,
I've happened to know some of his friends
very well, and from what they've told me
it ain't difficult for me to guess what'd be
the effect on him of meetin' you in one of
his hold-ups.   He's a passionate admirer of
beauty, and—you're the most beautiful
woman I've ever seen.''

" That's an A No. 1,'' said Jerroray, with

frank pleasure. "And I should like to remark that you ain't any slouch yourself,"
she added, by way of the retort courteous.
"I don't believe even Tom Nelson can beat
you on looks."

"I am afraid we'll none of us stand any
chance after you've once seen Mr. Nelson,"
said Jack Potts, with a deep sigh. "Good-
by—I must go. Think of me sometimes
kindly, for I will never forget you." He
took her hand as before, and this time kissed
it gallantly in addition to the pressure, and
as he looked at her for a final moment before he let it drop there was the same bold
significance in his eyes, under which hers
sank, while a vivid blush overspread her
face.

"Did Mr. Chance ever make you blush?"
he asked, in a low voice.

"No," she replied, with averted looks,
"nor any other feller. I don't like it."

Mr. Potts laughed contentedly, and in another moment was gone. The Red Devil,
was in a particularly devilish mood after two
days in the stable, and quite refused at first
to submit to his new master's requirements,
but walked about on his hind legs, to Miss
Roray's extreme delight. Mr. Potts was

evidently an expert horseman, however, and soon had him in hand, and then set off at a strong gallop towards the western sun. Jerroray watched them with her nose flattened against the kitchen window, until they were too far away and the sun too dazzling for her to see them longer. Then she sat down on the wash-bench and clasped her hands about her knee, and looked at the old Irish woman, comfortably making pies in the cluttered, messy kitchen.

"Biddy," said the young lady, "so much never happened to me in all my life before as has happened in the last twenty-four hours."

"Mercy on us! You don't say so!" exclaimed Biddy. She had spent ten of the more impressionable years of her life in New England and spoke a mixed dialect.

"Yes," pursued Jerroray, "when I went away from here yesterday I was engaged to Charley Shore, but I ain't engaged to him any longer, and since then I've met three other gentlemen that I like awfully and—and I don't know which one of them I'm in love with."

"The Lord have pity on us!" exclaimed Biddy. She had abandoned her pies, and

stood with arms akimbo and mouth ajar, listening to this extraordinary heart history.

" Yes," pursued Jerroray, " and I'm very
much in love, too, a great deal more than
ever I was with Charley Shore, but I can't
for the life of me tell which one it is."

" Might it be any of thim gintlemen as
was here this afternoon ? "

" Yes, those two, and the polite train robber that held me up last night.   I told you
how perfectly lovely he was.   And this Mr.
Chance was at the ball, and he dances just
splendid, and I began to think I liked him
'most as well as the train robber.   And
Potts was on the train this mornin', and I
liked him, too—he was so awful fascinatin'
and funny I almost thought he was nicer'n
Chance even.   But then they all seemed to
think Chance was Tom Nelson, so if he was
two of 'em that settled it—I was in love
with him sure.   But now it looks as if he
ain't Nelson, and I like Potts better'n better—he's got such an awful takin' way with
him.   But Nelson himself may turn up
any time, and perhaps he'll be best of all.
So I'm just as mixed as I can be, Biddy,
and I don't know what to do.   What's
the fun of bein' in love if you don't know

who it's with? I call it right down tantal-
izin'.''

"So it is, Jerry, so it is. But I don't see
how you can do anythin' but wait for somethin' to straighten it out for ye. An' if one
of 'em does turn out to be yer train robber,
too, why, then that'll settle it best of any
way.''

"I'm afraid there's no such luck," said
Jerroray, with a deep sigh. "And it's so
tryin' not to know. You can't tell which
you want to be nicest to—you can't play
any one of 'em straight. I don't believe
a girl ever had three such elegant gentlemen-
friends all at once. Say, Biddy, let me help
you make pies and see if that won't clear
my mind up. Give me a big apron and let
me have the rollin' pin.''

Thus, when the sheriff and his posse arrived a few minutes later they found the sheriff's daughter so deeply engaged in culinary
pursuits that she paid scant attention to their
request for information about Mr. Chance.

"Chance? Oh, he went off ever so long
ago.''

"Which way? How long ago?''

"Oh, half an hour or an hour ago or so.
Which way did he go, Biddy?''

Biddy hadn't noticed : she was bakin'
pies.

"You'll have to ask Ernest. What you
want him for, anyway? Goin' to give him
a dinner-party? I'll contribute a strawberry '
pie to the entertainment." And Jerroray,
balancing a pie on her hand, laughed in her
father's face with an exasperating impudence
which appeared to gratify her parent quite
as much as the most filial deference could
have done.

"I knew she wouldn't tell on him," he
said proudly to his attendants. "Jerry's
always dead game."

CHAPTER X

Tom Norrie's spirits rose higher and higher the farther he rode over the wide prairie and the more he fell in with the swing of Folly's elastic, measured stride. He was completely in love with the beautiful mare before he had gone half a mile, and leaned forward often and patted her glistening, slender neck. Miss Folly only tossed her head, however, at these demonstrations of regard, and abated her gallop not one jot. She did condescend to turn one clean-cut little ear backwards to gather up the honeyed words that Tom poured into it, but there was a scornful look the while in her big, soft eye, as if she would say to him, " You must be a fool to think I like anyone but my own master to make love to me. You're just wasting your words, Mr. Chance, of Nebraska, but if it amuses you it certainly doesn't hurt me, and you really have rather a pleasant hand on my mouth. So long as you don't jerk me we'll be friendly, at least. It's something in your favor that you should know enough to appreciate that I'm one horse in ten thousand, as you just remarked.''

Tom judged that they were going at the rate of a mile in three minutes, and when ten minutes had passed drew the mare up and took a survey of the horizon. Ahead was a range of mountains, softening gradually in the afternoon light and apparently not very far away, while around him lay the great stretch of prairie, rolling a little as he rode over it, but looking in the distance as level as a summer sea. The Roray mansion and the little town behind it seemed still very near, but he was already familiar with the curious deceptions of the atmosphere on these high plains, and this did not disturb him. No one was in sight in his pursuit, or anywhere else on the prairie. He loosened his hand on the curb still more, pressed his heels gently against Folly's sides and started her off again. She gave her head a little toss and the rein a pull, as if in celebration of the extra freedom allowed her, and walked along a few moments with alert, forward ears, looking first to the one side and then to the other.

" That's it, you beauty," murmured Tom, encouragingly. " Make a good choice of your road and then stick to it."

Folly had now apparently made up her mind, and the decision seemed to awaken in it joyous anticipations or reminiscences, for with a wide, low shake of her head, which expressed complete abandonment to delight, and implicated her heels in a smart little sympathetic kick-up, she set off again, this time on a most inspiriting, fast trot, which covered the ground quite as rapidly as her previous gallop. She had changed their direction a good deal more toward the south, and Tom noticed that she hardly deviated at all from it, though with no evident path to guide her. He saw at considerable distances as they sped along one or two lonely ranches, and once they had to skirt a bit of high wire fence, but they saw not a single human being, far or near. Folly allowed herself a five minutes' walk after half an hour or more of steady trotting, and then went on at a somewhat less rapid gait, though with no evidence of diminished spirits or interest.

Tom's excitement was now a little cooled, and he began to review the events of the

last few hours, to wonder what was going to
happen to him, and to ask himself if he
should really go on and let Folly take him
to the destination she was bent on.   He
might so easily get out of the State instead,
thus escaping his danger altogether.   He let
his thoughts run on as to how he could
safely get the mare back to Jack Potts if he
did that and to what he should then do with
himself; but in the midst of his plans he
had a sudden revulsion of feeling, which
turned him right-about-face.

" The idea of giving it up now ! " he said
to himself.   " That would be a crazy thing
to do !   Here I am well in for a bona-fide
adventure, with half a dozen mysteries attached and unlimited future possibilities.
Get out of it?   Not much !   No matter
what the danger I may be running into, I
must go on now to satisfy my curiosity, if
for nothing else.   There are so many things
to be elucidated.   In the first place, what on
earth made these idiots think me Tom Nelson ?   And then why should Jack Potts,
after six hours' acquaintance, care to take
the trouble to get me out of their clutches ?
Perhaps he thinks I'm Tom Nelson, too, in
spite of his saying I wasn't.   By George,

that must be it ! " and Tom found much corroboration for this theory as he ran in his mind over all that had happened, and remembered Mr. Potts's peculiar and persistent smile.

" He seemed taken with Jerroray—greatly taken. Possibly he just wished to get me out of her way. But then how in the devil did he have this clever beast so handy ? He can't keep horses in every town he visits. Could the Keaches, with their names all parted in the middle, have got the nag for him ? " And Tom befogged his brain in vain attempts to explain Mr. Jack Potts and his abundant resources, equine and otherwise. " Folly's been this road many a time before, or she'd not go it so true and steady. Oh, you pretty blackbird," he said to her in a caressing voice, " if I knew all you know I should be a good deal wiser than I am."

He looked his pistols over carefully, and congratulated himself on having lately acquired the habit of wearing them. He tore his mutilated handkerchief into shreds and left it on the plain behind him, while he regarded with a grimace one of the substitutes he had purchased in Aurora. He remembered his " boiled shirts " in the extension

bag at the hotel, each with a neat red T. N.
on the tab in front. "What a fool I was to
travel around with such give-aways as that!
Anyhow there's not an initial on my present
outfit, and nothing to make Tom Nelson, if
he met me, think I had $700 aboard. And
I'm not a half bad shot with the revolver, as
my competitors found in the late shooting
match at Titus City; and, besides, not
really caring a cent what may happen to me,
I sha'n't be nervous. And if my being taken
for Tom Nelson could by any possibility end
in my making that gentleman's acquaintance
—well, I'd ask nothing better. Hurrah for
Folly!" he suddenly shouted aloud, wav-
ing his hat over his head. "Wisdom to the
wall forever!"

Folly took these demonstrations as an in-
dication that more speed was required of
her, and leaped into a run in about a second's time. Tom had never ridden so fast
in his life, and he held his breath with delight in it. "Gently, my bird—gently,
my beauty," he said, drawing her up at last.
"Don't wind yourself, for so far as I can
see we aren't getting anywhere at all, and
you've still a good deal of a road before
you."

The mountains ahead, which looked so near at the start, seemed somehow scarcely any nearer yet, but a long spur extended out into the plain, parallel with Folly's route, detaching itself in more vivid color from the rest of the range, and seeming almost close enough to hit with a stone. Tom calculated, however, that it was fully five miles distant, if not more ; while ahead there might still be fifteen or twenty miles before the plain gave way to the mountain. Suddenly there was a dip in the ground, and across their path lay a sluggish stream, winding away to the south. Folly quickened her pace and made straight for the edge of the creek, at a spot where the marks of many hoofs indicated a ford. They were soon on the other side, and then the mare turned almost at right angles and went off with renewed speed towards the nearer spur of the mountains. No signs of human life were visible yet, even when they were close under the edge of the hill, but they struck a trail which took them up and around it, and brought them into a wooded ravine, and then all at once they arrived at a camp and were greeted by the baying of a melancholy hound. Folly trotted across the rough clearing to a long shed that was evidently her stable, and answered politely the loud and enthusiastic whinnies that saluted her from within.   In an instant a man appeared from another long, low building above, which had eight or ten front doors opening on a common porch.   As he slouched down the hill Tom jumped off and stood waiting with a pleasant smile, but the man neither looked at him nor responded to his greeting. He opened a door and 'led Folly inside the shed, where he proceeded to remove her gear and rub her down, leaving Tom to take care of himself as he might choose.

Tom, with his hands in his pockets, looked in at the open door.   "She needs a good rubbing," he said.   "She's come a long distance splendidly."

The man only grunted in an irritated way, and finally, when Tom followed up one or two similar observations with a request to be informed where he should go, his new acquaintance suggested that he'd better go to hell, and be quick about it, too.

Thus admonished, our hero strolled up the hill, with his eye watchfully on the long cabin, within whose many front doors seemed to lie infinite possibilities.   Would

his host be as sweet-tempered as the hostler,
he wondered, or was the amiable hostler
perhaps his host? He knocked on the first
door, and receiving no answer, moved on to
the second, where his knock was followed
by one grunt, two snores, and the sound of
a person asleep turning over in bed. Then
he knocked on the third door, which flew
open, while an indignant red head and a revolver appeared. Tom began hurriedly to
explain, but the owner of the red head was
evidently no more interested in his conversation than the other man had been.

"Pete—I say, Pete!" he called out
down the hill, and, on Pete's appearance,
"Where'd this d——d nuisance come from,
and why hain't you shot him?"

"Come in on the black mare just now.
I don't shoot folks without orders," said
Pete.

"Well, lock him up in the kennel, then;
he's bound to wake us all up and keep us
awake. Fling him a bone to keep him quiet,
if it's grub he wants, and we'll use him for a
target bimeby, when we're ready to amuse
ourselves." The red head was decorated
with a fiendish grin as it uttered these words,
and the revolver was held so that Tom

looked straight into its shining muzzle. He caught himself wondering, as he did so, why he was not more alarmed.

" I'm only a passenger," he observed, with irresponsible cheerfulness.

" And therefore to be held up," said the red-headed gentleman, sententiously.

" Is that the necessary order of entertainment?" Tom ventured to inquire.

" What sort of d——d entertainment do you expect in a Den of Thieves?" inquired a bearded monster, who had apparently been impelled by curiosity to come and look over the red-headed man's shoulder.

" Oh—a Den of Thieves," said Tom, a little weakly.

" Yes, a Den of Thieves," returned the new-comer, fiercely. " Got anything to say to that? Any criticisms to offer? Spit 'em out quick if you have."

" Oh, no—none at all—none at all," said Mr. Norrie, with elaborate politeness. " On the contrary, it sounds very charming—er— forty thieves?" he inquired.

" Never you mind how many," said the bearded gentleman.

" Enough to make you into bloomin' hash," added the red-headed one.

" I was only thinking," explained Tom cordially, " that if they're all as agreeable as you two gentlemen, there couldn't be too many. And I was hoping I should meet them all as soon as possible. Of course I'm excessively sorry I waked you up, but I wouldn't have missed the pleasure of making your acquaintance for anything." Tom had been gazing pretty intently at the revolver so far, but was conscious, at the same time, of the appearance of several other human beings on the porch ; and now, somewhat accustomed to the perils of his situation, allowed himself to look about. A Chinaman and an albino boy regarded him from one side, and from the door above, where he had heard the snores, three more men had come out, and were looking on with interest.

" Don't scare worth a d—n, does he, Gully ? " said one of these new-comers, a tall, hulking, large-boned boy.

" Well, he ain't quite such a lady as he looks," admitted the red-headed Gully, uncocking his pistol, and putting it in his belt.

" We'll put up a show later that'll terrorize him some," threatened the black-bearded man, whom the others addressed as Snide.

"It don't agree with me to be waked up, and it don't agree any better with the d—n fool that does it." Snide stepped out on the porch, stretched himself, and yawned loudly with the abandon of a big animal.

The yawn proved infectious, and after the others had gone through the same process they all sat down on the bench that ran along the porch and talked the situation over. They discussed Tom and his appearance with as much frankness as if he hadn't been there, or as if he were a curiosity in a cage. They pawed him over and emptied his pockets, possessing themselves of his pistols, his watch, and some thirty dollars in his purse, while he blessed himself inwardly for having concealed the large amount of ready money that he carried in a place beyond their conjecture.

"He don't wear no money belt," declared Gully, feeling of Tom's waist with suspicious care. "Guess he ain't blessed with a large amount of plunks."

Gully had passed on Tom's wallet, after emptying all the money out, to the ungainly boy, who answered indiscriminately to the names of Baby, Bub, Trilby, Girlie, and a few others. This engaging youth had since

been industriously exploring the papers which
it contained, and now gave a whoop of delight and waved Janet's picture in the air.
Tom had to endure the agony of seeing him
kiss it, press it dramatically to his heart, and
otherwise carry on with it in a way that
made Mr. Norrie anxious to punch his head
in.   The others all admired it, and allowed
that she was " a neat gal," but the obnoxious Trilby did not cease to talk about it,
and produced it frequently from his breast
pocket for further offensive attentions.   Mr.
Norrie forced himself to look amiable and
easy throughout this ordeal, but he registered a vow that Trilby should pay well for
his impudence if he ever got out of his present predicament.   " He's a heavy lout,"
thought Tom, " but he looks as if he couldn't
manage himself much better than a mastiff
puppy.   Wonder if I've forgotten how to
wrestle ? "

Tom's few attempts to join pleasantly in
the conversation were discouraged with peremptory suggestions to shut up, and not be
too fresh, enforced by still more peremptory
revolvers.   When he hoped to secure more
courteous treatment by telling them of his
friend, Mr. Jack Potts, their hilarity was

great, and they made an endless number of
puns and jokes, with Mr. Potts's name as a
basis and the game of poker to ring the
changes on.   They represented themselves
as entirely unacquainted with any Jack Potts,
and were sure that they didn't want him for
a friend, if this was the pokerish sort of a
trick he played on those he loved.   Tom,
indeed, looking on their villainous faces—
Snide was easily quite his ideal of a mur-
derer and a cut-throat, and some of the
others looked hardly less evil—began seriously to doubt the sincerity of Mr. Potts's
intentions, and to wonder a little forlornly
what would be the outcome of the great
trust he had reposed in that perfidious gentleman.   His possession of the black mare,
and the black mare's bee line from Aurora
to the Den of Thieves, were more than ever
unfathomable mysteries in the light of his
not being himself known in that attractive
resort.   On a sudden impulse he asked whose
horse Folly was, but regretted it bitterly
when at once they greeted him with cheers
as a jolly horse thief.

"Say, ain't you a little green, though?"

"She's your horse, ain't she, if you tuck
her?"

" Did you shoot the man or trick him ? "

" Guess you knew where you was comin',
arter all, when you made for the Den of
Thieves."

Our hero was immensely relieved when
the red-eyed boy finally announced that
" breakfus " was ready, and they all moved
on down the porch to what they called the
" grub-room," where the Chinaman cooked
and served their meals.

They made a long evening of it after the
" breakfast," with plenty to drink, and Tom
as a butt for jokes. As they grew more hilarious they actually set him up as a target,
and fired bullets around him with great dex-
terity. They were so drunk by this time
that Tom was more frightened than he had
been at all, but he managed to conceal his
emotions under a fairly cool manner, and
they soon tired of the pursuit. At last, real-
izing perhaps, that they were not in the
best condition to guard him, they gave the
grim Pete orders to put him to bed, and Tom
turned in in the " kennel," which was by no
means so bad as its name, with a great sense
of thankfulness that he still kept a whole
skin.

Among other valuable accomplishments

acquired since he had so suddenly retired from business, Mr. Norrie had learned to sleep well, and in spite of the ticklishness of his situation and the great racket set up by the merry-makers close by, he was off in a very few minutes. His long ride across the plains and the late hour of the ball at Bud only the night before, though it seemed to him a week since, contributed to keep him from being troubled by insomnia, and it was thus high noon before he awoke the next day.

The stout door of the kennel, which Pete had locked as he left him, now stood open, and there was a pleasant hum of insects and twitter of birds in the warm sunshine outside. Our hero was wide awake in an instant, recalling all that happened the previous night, and at once got up and looked warily out on the porch. With a thrill of joy he saw Jack Potts calmly sitting there and smoking his pipe. Down the hill Pete was rubbing off one horse, while several others stood about in the shade, switching their tails, and at the kitchen end of the cabin the Chinaman and the boy were moving in and out about their domestic labors. No one else was visible, though a

13

sound of voices came from one of the rooms beyond.

Jack Potts suddenly heard something, and turned quickly. " Oh, it's you," he said. " Good-morning, Mr. Chance. Want some breakfast first, or a pipe ? "

" I had my breakfast at five o'clock tea last night," said Tom, sitting down on the edge of the porch.

" And prefer to dine on the following day? Well, Yung Wun's getting dinner for us all, so that'll just suit. You look happy."

" I feel so," said Tom. " I was never so glad to see anybody in my life."

Mr. Potts smiled. " How'd you like Tom Nelson ? " he inquired.

" Tom Nelson ? " said Tom Norrie, aghast. " I haven't seen Tom Nelson."

" Sure of that ? " asked Jack Potts, calmly.

" Good Lord ! he can't be one of those villains that entertained me last night ! "

" Think not ? What did they do to you ? "

Mr. Chance, of Nebraska, narrated feelingly his experiences in the Den of Thieves, while Jack Potts continued to smile.

" And you didn't recognize Tom Nel-

son ? '' he asked.   '' I supposed you'd see
through his disguise the first thing.''

Tom was thoroughly puzzled.   Gully ?
Snide ? Trilby ? The others ? None of them
could be Tom Nelson.   Wild thoughts even
came into his head of the Chinaman and the
albino boy.

'' Well, if you care anything about meetin' Mr. Nelson,'' continued Jack Potts, '' he
was in that room yonder a few minutes ago.
You'd better go along and inquire for him.
He's been told of the interest you take in
him, and he's much flattered.''

Tom rose a little reluctantly.   Now that
he was so near the object of his desire
he suddenly felt that it was all very flat.
'' Won't you come along and introduce
me ? '' he asked, but Jack Potts shook his
head.

'' Tom Nelson is an old story to me,'' he
said, '' and I'm very comfortable here.''

So Tom walked along the porch and in at
the open door which Mr. Potts had signified.
Snide was sitting there alone, his feet on the
table and a pipe in his mouth.

'' Hullo,'' he said to himself reflectively,
'' here's the bloomin' target again.   Wonder
what he wants ? ''

" I want to see Tom Nelson," said Tom.

" Well I've no objections.   See him all you want to ? "

" Can you tell me where I can find him ? "

" I dessay I could—if I wanted to.   Tain't against the law to look for him," and Snide pointed over his shoulder with his thumb to a door opening into the room beyond.

Tom passed through it, and came upon the boy, Gully, and Button, one of the other men, playing at poker, while the fifth member of the gang, known as Jinks, or, if you wished to be especially polite, High Jinks, was visible in the next room, sound asleep on one of the so-called beds.

" Good-morning," said Tom, politely.

" Oh—goodby," responded Gully with equal urbanity.

" Is—is Tom Nelson here ? " asked Tom, feeling flatter than ever.

" Didn't you hear what Gully said ? " demanded Trilby with an ugly frown.   " We're havin' a quiet little game and don't want to be interrupted."

" Jack Potts told me to look in here for Tom Nelson," said Tom, even more weakly, but returning Trilby's frown with one equally malignant.   He felt a strong desire to

pitch the ungainly boy out of the door, only
that at this moment the figure of Mr. Potts
appeared in it.

" Always do as yer bid ? " inquired Trilby
offensively, unsuspicious of his danger.

" An who's this yer Jack Potts you're forever talkin' about? " demanded Gully. " I'm
sick of him, I am. We don't know no Potts
round here, and we don't want to. You just
shut up on Potts from now on."

" Gully's sensitive about jack-pots," observed Trilby, with a grin.   " He's lost three
since we begun playin'."

" Well, don't get quarrellin' about it the
way you did last week," suggested Mr. Potts.
" Another such row as that wouldn't be very
good for your health, Bub, or for Gully's
either."

There was a quiet tone of authority in Mr.
Potts's voice, and Bub looked sulky instead of
answering back.   A sudden idea dawned on
Tom Norrie's mind.   Then for about ten
seconds that organ was worked so actively in
reminiscence confirmatory of the new idea
that it would hardly be amiss to say that his
brain whirled.

" Great Heavens ! " he exclaimed. " And
to think that it never entered my head before.

Well, I have been what Jerroray would cal
a plumb idiot ! ''   He looked at his smiling
friend in the doorway.   '' That's why you
smiled all the time, wasn't it ? ''

    '' It was a good enough joke, don't you
think ? ''

    '' I should rise to observe,'' declared Tom.
'' Allow me to shake hands with you. Whatever we may think about the right or wrong
of your profession, Mr. Nelson, your daring
and wit combined beat anything since the
days of Robin Hood, and I am proud to
know you.   In short you exceed my highest
expectations ! ''

    Tom Nelson and Tom Norrie shook hands
in a most friendly manner, while the others
looked on, Snide having walked in grinning
from the other room, and the sleeper being
wakened for the occasion with a chair shied
at him by Gully.

    '' Now, gentlemen,'' said Tom Nelson,
'' havin' had your own fun with Mr. Chance
last night, suppose this morning you return
him his property.''

    This was done very good-naturedly, until
it came Trilby's turn, and he sulkily produced the soiled photograph.

    '' You and I have an account to settle,''

said Tom. "If I can't give you a good thrashing I'll at least have a try at it."

"Bub needs one bad enough," said Tom Nelson, "and I'll thank you if you succeed in givin' it to him. Meanwhile let's waive all unpleasantness and eat our dinner. Yung Wun announces that it's ready."

CHAPTER XI

Tom was an inmate of the outlaw's camp for more than a week. The fact that he was a prisoner was not made obvious, but he knew well that he should not be allowed to get away, and that if he tried he might pay for the attempt with his life. But his treatment at the hands of Nelson was that of a distinguished and congenial guest. The two young men were together almost continuously, and for the most part out of doors, while the other members of the gang, crowded in one of the small rooms or "caves," as they called them, of the den, played poker from morning until night, and quarrelled as they played.

Mixed as Tom's feelings might be in other directions, he was in no sort of doubt about his liking for Tom Nelson, and he thoroughly enjoyed this close intercourse with him. To his other charms Nelson added that of great candor, and related the events of his career to our hero with most gratifying frankness.

" Are you going to shoot me before you're through with me ? " inquired Tom, "or why, otherwise, do you entrust me with all these damaging secrets ? "

" You're the first civilized bein' I've been on intimate terms with for about three years, for one thing," said Nelson, "and your appreciative interest warms my heart. For another thing, I contemplate retirin' from my business, as you've done from yours, and when I've skipped it would be difficult to find me. Besides, I'm rarely mistaken in men, and I'd stake anythin' on your not betrayin' me—even to get yourself out of a tight hole."

Tom Nelson, by his own account, was the scapegrace son of a Chicago millionaire and "self-made" man. This gentleman, having succeeded so admirably, as he thought, in the manufacture of himself, had rendered his wife miserable for a matter of a quarter of a century or so, in a determined attempt to improve on the handiwork of Providence and fashion her over in his own image. Failing quite in giving to the poor

lady those methodical and saving habits and
that hard singleness of mind to which he at-
tributed his great success, he nevertheless set
about the rearing of his only son in these
habits and this mind, according to a cast-
iron recipe made up from his experience.
He was a hard man and his rule was hard.
He allowed no leeway and never overlooked
a fault.   Tom, too spirited to stand this
treatment, ran away from home at fourteen,
but was brought back after a week or two of
vicissitudinous freedom, and promised his
mother, whom he loved, that he would try
thereafter to bear everything for her sake,
and stay by her as her support and comfort.
If his mother had lived she might, through
his love for her, have made a useful man of
him, for he had undeniable talents.   But
she died before he was eighteen, her heart
broken by the long struggle with John Nelson's cold disapproval.   Tom and his father
quarrelled for three or four years longer, until at last Tom was expelled from Harvard
in the middle of his second year there, and
then the elder Nelson broke entirely with
his son and left him to shift for himself.

" Lucky day for me when the old skin-
flint cast me off," said the outlaw, having

narrated the story of his life up to this point
with full details. " He used me like a dog.
There weren't half a dozen fellers in Harvard College whose fathers had so much
money as mine, and there weren't half a
dozen fellers who had so little to spend
themselves. I had to get money by hook or
by crook, and, of course, it led me into bad
ways. I was always in scrapes from the
time I was a little tacker, and they were all
owing to the fact that I hadn't money
enough, and was too proud to admit that
my father wouldn't give it to me. He kept
poor mother so tight, making her render a
strict account of everything, that she had
to falsify her accounts in order to get me a
single cent. Dear old mother! She was a
good 'nough Christian to do it, too. If it
hadn't been for her I'd be a good deal
worse villain than I am. But when the his-
torians of my career inquire into my school
life in Chicago, at Exeter, and finally at
Harvard, they'll remark that anyone could
easily have foretold the end, for my record's
pretty black wherever I went. And when
Dad said good-by to me, three years ago, I
supplemented his sanctimonious partin' advice, which was all he gave me to start me

in my tussle with the world, by breakin'
into the house the next night, holdin' him
up and makin' him fork over the contents
of his safe.   I can tell you, the old gent was
scared blue !   I was ugly, and he knew it,
and he didn't like the looks of my revolver,
so he walks downstairs in his night-shirt,
without peepin,' and undoes his old safe and
meekly hands over the needful, and I came
off into the bloomin' West with somethin'
besides advice for an outfit.   My farewell
present to him was the assurance that whatever I did—and he agreed with me that I
was likely to accomplish somethin' pretty
disgraceful—I'd do under the name of Nelson, and advertise, too, whose son I was,
and how he used my mother.   He's had
several pleasant little messages from me since
in his mornin' paper.   You know," he declared with great earnestness, " I'd like so
to spite him the worst way that I'm 'most
ready to let myself be caught and go to
jail."
   " That all explains," said Tom, " why
everybody knows your name—a circumstance
that struck me as peculiar when I first began
to hear about you."
   " Yes.   I'm a train robber for somethin'

besides the emoluments. I'm a train robber for revenge—I'm payin' back a man I hate for all he did to me and my mother," and Mr. Nelson's face wore an expression it was not pleasant to see. " The more notoriety I can give to the name of Nelson the better it suits me," he went on, "and you can bet it's got a lot in the last three years. And I've had money enough, too, for the first time in my life, and had a d——d good time out of it. I'll miss the fun and excitement when I've given it up," he added, with a sigh. "I know I sha'n't enjoy a blameless life."

Tom laughed. " Is that the necessary program ? " he asked. " And why ? "

Tom Nelson sighed still more deeply. " Spoons on a girl," he said. " Can't ask her to go into this business with me."

" Pity it isn't Jerroray," said Tom. " She'd be delighted with the business, and would like nothing better than to go train robbing on her wedding tour ! "

" Think so ? " said the other Tom carelessly.

" Well, you ought to have heard her talk about you that night at Bud, if you doubt it. And you know when you joined our afternoon tea with the announcement that I was suspected of being the great Mr. Nelson, she grew sweet on me in no time. She squeezed my hand on the back steps, and I've felt ever since that I lost one of the opportunities of my life in not kissing her. I know she would have let me do it."

" You hadn't any time to spare," observed Mr. Nelson, as if the conversation didn't interest him much.

" But she'd be very nice sweet kissing all the same," persisted Tom. " I never saw a complexion like hers—she looks luscious enough to eat."

" How about the girl in the photograph for whose sake you wiped up the corral with Bub and yourself alternately, and got yourself that superior black eye ? "

" Well, I licked the odious Infant," declared Tom.

" Yes—but how about the girl ? "

" Oh, she's dark," said Tom. " Dark women never have complexions like Jerroray's—or light ones, either, for that matter."

" But you like her, don't you ? Else why should you smash poor Bub into such a jelly ? "

" I'd have smashed Bub all the same if it had been a girl I didn't know. He's the most obnoxious young man I ever met. Nothing ever happened to me that did me so much good as beating him. I was afraid he was too heavy for me."

" So he was," said the outlaw, " but you had the most brains. You beat him by brains. It was a fine thing to see."

Tom smiled with pleasure at this tribute.

" I wish that girl could have seen it," added Nelson, artfully. " She'd have liked you then, even if you don't like her."

" Ah, no, that's just the trouble," said Tom, gloomily, falling into the trap. " I like her much better than she likes me."

" Oh, pooh—she's foolin' you, as girls always do," said Mr. Nelson. " She couldn't help likin' you."

Whereupon our hero, as his astute friend desired, told him all about Janet and his late sad experience with her, and found it delightful to unburden his heart to so sympathetic a listener. " I've never spoken of this to a soul before," he said. " I don't know why I should tell you."

" Because I wanted so much to know," said Tom Nelson, with sudden hilarity.

"You've made me a very happy man. I was afraid you were my serious rival with Jerroray, but you can't be in love with two girls at once."

Tom rose gravely and shook hands with Nelson. "I offer you my congratulations on having placed your affections upon one of the most interesting and attractive young women I ever met," he said. "And since you are really Tom Nelson, as well as the agreeable Jack Potts, you will have no difficulty in winning her, for her heart is romantic and her imagination is greatly fired by your exploits. And I venture to predict that, however tame and blameless a life you may lead, with Jerroray as a companion you will never find it insipid. Boredom could not exist alongside her. And in twenty years she will be even handsomer than she is now."

Nelson returned his handshake with feeling. "This does my heart good," he said. "She is a peach—now isn't she?"

"She's a most superlative peach," declared Tom. "A California peach, a peach of the finest bloom and rarest flavor. I envy you unspeakably its lifelong consumption!" Tom Nelson stared at him upon this last remark. "But—but the other girl?"

"If I could have won Jerroray I should
have forgotten the other girl in five minutes," said Tom Norrie, very gloomily. For
the time being he actually thought it. All
the possible embarrassments of marriage to
Jerroray vanished from his mind, and he
dwelt with regret upon her abundant charms.
Janet—well, Janet was far away, and had
jilted him besides. And then she was too
staid, too Eastern, to live the Bohemian life
he meant to live hereafter, and it would just
have suited Jerroray. And Jerroray liked
him, too. By an ardent pursuit he might
perhaps have turned that liking into something more tender and more deep. How
adorable it would have been to be the object of her frank and artless affection! He
felt himself a blighted being in good earnest
and sentimentally gloated in it, as all genuine blighted beings must ever do. But it
was eminently in accord with the novel situation in which he found himself that he
should chivalrously resign his pretensions in
favor of the robber lord, who, if not his
feudal superior, was certainly his superior in
arms and equipment and an excellent fellow
to boot. "It is better that you should have
her," he said, generously. "You are more

14

fitted to make her happy.'' This original
sentiment pleased him. He remembered
that in plays the villain always said it to the
hero in the last act, and was glad that he
happened to think of it so appropriately.
'' I suppose you'll have a church wedding at
Aurora and the Terror to give his daughter
away?'' he asked with courageous cheerfulness.

'' I prefer quiet weddin's,'' said Nelson,
with a smile. '' I don't think we'll ask the
sheriff.''

'' I hope it may be soon,'' said Tom.
'' She must get herself a superior wedding
present with the stakes of our wager, for
you've won not only that, but everything
else—half a dozen jack-pots to bless your
lucky choice of a name.''

'' You know that wager wasn't fair,'' said
Mr. Nelson. '' If it had been arranged the
ordinary way I should have given you back
your money, of course.''

'' I'd far rather the bride should have it,''
said Tom.

'' It's funny the change of feelin' I went
through about you,'' continued Nelson, in
a reminiscent tone. '' I haven't told you
what a narrow escape you had. I don't

quite know that I want to now even, for
since I know you and like you so well it
seems a d——d snide trick to have thought
of playin' on you.''

But Tom's curiosity was strongly roused,
and he became so urgent in his petitions for
information that presently the outlaw began
to tell his tale, his countenance decorated
with the little characteristic smile of inward
amusement that from the first Tom had
found so attractive. And as he went on in
his narrative of the events of the last two
days our hero listened with a more and more
absorbed attention, becoming painfully aware
of how much may be happening about the
ears of complacent simplicity and never
even be suspected thereby. And yet he had
thought himself so sharp !

It seemed that Nelson had a taste for
knowing what people thought about him, no
matter how dangerous the pursuit of such
knowledge might be. Four times had he
made trips through Rising Sun and Creosote
Counties in his character of a jewelry drummer—once before his career as an outlaw
opened, once directly after the first hold-up,
and the third time a fortnight later. His
adventures had been picturesque, and he

had overheard or joined in very entertaining conversations anent Mr. Nelson and his exploits.   He had amused himself by artlessly fostering the incipient tendency to "take pride" in that noted outlaw, and had seized eagerly at the excellent chance he saw to make the train robber a popular character with the masses.   Like an actor, he had learned from the people themselves where he could best make his "points" with them, and had put in practice cleverly all the suggestions they innocently gave him.

His arrival at Bud the morning after the ball, however, following so soon upon his last visit there, and thus likely to arouse suspicion in the minds of reflecting men, had there been any men at all given to reflection, was brought about solely by an interest in Miss Roray.   The ingenuous humor of her appeal to him when he held her up, had entertained him greatly, and the more he thought about her the more anxious he was to have another glimpse of her and see if she were really so attractive and original as she seemed.   But before he saw her again he had seen Tom, in the office of the Empire Hotel—as heretofore narrated.

"I suppose you haven't frequented post-

offices much out here?" he asked, suddenly, at this juncture.

"No, I haven't been in one that I know
of. Why?" counter-questioned Tom Norrie, carelessly.

"I thought you weren't aware that your
family and friends have advertised you as
'disappeared,' giving a full description of
you, of course, and offering a reward for information about you."

Our hero emitted an ejaculation of surprise and disgust.

"At least, it's in the one at Bud, where
I 'ad just been that mornin', and with my
accustomed curiosity I had happened to
read it through. I noticed that you had
disappeared over ten days before the first of
our robberies, which somehow struck me as
an interestin' fact, and that you 'ad been at
Harvard two or three years before I was.
And when I saw you half an hour later in
the hotel office at Bud I suspected in an
instant that you were Thomas Norrie, Jr.,
even before I saw the initials on your handkerchief. As you may remember, my back
was turned when you came into the room,
and so I heard you speak before I saw you.
Your voice was so like my father's, and also

as I knew, like my own, that it startled me. While you talked with Dicker I stared at you, awestruck with the fatality of the whole thing. We didn't look alike in face, but we were almost identical in size and physique—and as no one, of course, had seen Tom Nelson's face there was absolutely no obstacle that I could see to palmin' you off as myself. The jealousy of Mr. Shore and the other young men over your success with the fair Jerry helped me out wonderfully, and there wasn't a man in the car didn't feel sure you were I by the time we reached Aurora. It was the quickest and neatest thing in the world, a perfect train of circumstantial evidence, and you as innocent of it all as an infant! In short, there was only one out in the whole thing.''

''And what, pray, was that?'' inquired Tom, dryly.

'' The fact that I'd taken a most untimely and inconvenient shine to you,'' declared Nelson. '' If it hadn't been for that, you'd now be languishin' in Aurora jail, with state-prison before you.''

'' Oh, hardly,'' protested Tom. '' They could never have convicted me, you know.

My people would have come on to identify me.''

'' But your people hadn't seen you since the 25th of April, and our first hold-up didn't take place till the 6th of May.''

'' But I was somewhere else on the 6th of May.''

'' Of course,'' said Nelson. '' But could you prove it satisfactorily to any jury?'' He pointed out succinctly to Mr. Norrie the inborn distrust of the Western juryman for alibis, and reminded him of the unpromising character of his associates since he had come from the East, which would make it the more easy to suspect that their testimony had been bought for the occasion. And when he asked Tom if he remembered where he was, and the names of the men he was with on the three important dates, Tom was surprised to find how hazy was his recollection of details.

But in spite of his being obliged thus to admit that he had had rather a narrow squeak of it, his sentiments towards the outlaw were entirely of gratitude for his having saved him rather than of resentment for his getting him into such a scrape. In short, Tom Nelson was a man of great fascination,

and Tom Norrie found it far easier to like
him and succumb to his charm than to disapprove of him and resist.   It seemed indeed impossible to disapprove of so light-
hearted and gay a villain, on whom his vil-
lainy sat with so gracious an air of irresponsible youth.   Tom often wondered
about it, and finally came to the conclusion
that the reason he could not think of him
as a bad man, was that the outlaw did not
think of himself as one.   He simply had no
moral sense.   The fact that the world, as
represented by his father, had used him
hard, was in his mind excuse enough for all
that he cared to do in retaliation.   Circumstances had made him a train robber and he
got great fun out of his risky profession,
while his conscience slept so peacefully that
Tom was inclined to argue that he hadn't
any.   As Tom had somehow felt in his smile
and the tone of his voice, the first morning
that he saw him, all life was merely an entertaining joke to him, and it was by no means
the poorest part of the joke to hold up train
after train in exactly the same region, to
travel about in the most reckless way imaginable and never to get caught.   And there
could be no more fitting wind-up to the joke

than to marry the sheriff's daughter under
the sheriff's very nose and leave for parts
unknown—which, it seemed, was Mr. Nelson's present program if he could secure
the lady's consent.

Nor could Tom anticipate shipwreck for
this extraordinary marriage, should it ever be
" arranged." In the first place, how could
two people, each so unusually attractive,
ever fall out of love with each other, having
once fallen in? And if this logic were dis-
proved by the notorious facts of matrimony, there were two even, easy tempers, two
excellent common senses, and two superior
senses of humor to fall back upon. They
would have such a good time, such a jolly
time, all the time, that there would never be
any leisure time in which to repent. Nor
would matrimony lose its charm in settled
domesticity—they could not be domestic or
settled if they tried. Bohemia would always
claim them for its own, and impart to their
roving ménage—it was sure to be roving—
its own delicious touch of eternal youth.
Mossiness might be picturesque on rocks and
stones, thought Tom, but surely on human
beings it was generally synonymous with dull
priggishness and narrow minds, and that

fatal flavor of bread and butter which he hated more than anything else. For his own daily food the human rolling-stones, with all these accumulations of settled conventional prejudice knocked off by contact with the world, and their corners and excrescences smoothed down into comfortable livableness, were the apples of gold and silver, and his ideal of what he wished himself to be to others. He looked back upon the man he had been, only a few short weeks before, when Janet had jilted him, and did not wonder at what she had done. He, too, jilted that gone-by Tom Norrie; but the new one, with a new philosophy of life, or rather an old philosophy long dimly apprehended, but only now put into practice, was not half a bad sort of fellow. " Could Janet ever be made to think so? " he asked himself, and mournfully shook his head.

Another hold-up occurred while Tom Norrie was residing at the Den of Thieves. Three of the gang rode off one morning, and Nelson with the other two departed in the afternoon. Pete, silent and irritable as ever, became omnipresent after they had gone, and Tom found it impossible to get out of his sight. He submitted quietly

to this espionage, and was locked into the
kennel as usual at bedtime.

But though not taken into Mr. Nelson's
confidence beforehand, he was told all about
the affair the next day.   It had been a more
than usually successful and also a more than
usually exciting raid.   The train was a
through express from the East, with some
rich travellers on it, and there had been
many amusing incidents of their unwilling-
ness to part with their belongings.

Among other such tales Nelson related the
following :—" There were several pretty
girls aboard, but one in partic'lar that could
see 'em all and go 'em easily ten or twenty
better, and she was as plucky as she was
pretty, and mad clear through.   You ought
to have seen her eyes flash at me.   ' Your
money or your life,' I says very politely.
' I'll give you nothin',' says she.   ' Anything you want of mine you'll take by main
force or not at all.'   So I proceeded, as
gently as possible, to take possession of a
small satchel she carried, which proved to
have a lot of money and jewelry in it.   She
didn't struggle a bit, but simply hung on,
and looked all the time straight at me, with
set lips and a big frown.   ' I never wished

I was a man before,' says she, ' and if I had my revolver here I wouldn't now.' ' Can you shoot straight?' says I. 'I'd be very glad to show you if you'd lend me your pistol and act as a target?' she answered, quick as flash. ' On the whole I'm afraid it wouldn't be quite safe,' says I. ' Somehow you look as if you'd hit, and I don't think I care to be hit to-day. But if ever we should meet again———' ' We will meet again, I hope, and in a court of law,' says she, ' and I'll be a good witness for the prosecution.' The old lady with her tried to stop her all the time, loadin' me down with her own belongin's and tryin' to get round me and smooth things over, but the girl's blood was up, and she had to speak her mind. I liked her for it, too. Folks seem to think courage is all for the men, but it seems to me it suits women just as well. None of your shrinkin' little misses for me ! ''

" The modern girl never shrinks," observed Mr. Norrie.

Tom Nelson was a born story-teller and went on with his yarns until Tom Norrie's spirit was thoroughly fired.

" By George, it must be fun," he said, spontaneously. " I wish I'd been there ! ''

Nelson turned quickly. " Do you really?" he asked. "If I'd known that I'd have taken you. I was afraid you had scruples."

" Well, so I have, I suppose," laughed Tom. " But I must say I wouldn't mind looking on and participating in the fun— though not in the boodle."

"I'd like you to see a hold-up in our best style," said the outlaw, with a note of reflection in his voice. " I had sort of an idea we'd make this the last, but hang it all, it's such good fun that I always want one more try before I give it up. I'll have an-other, too, and take you along, be d——d if I won't."

" Oh, come," said Tom, "don't make me responsible. I don't want you to hold up trains to entertain me."

" Don't you worry. It's me that's doin' it, and I'm glad of any excuse for it," said Nelson. "It's like gamblin'—there's so much risk in it I can't make up my mind to let it alone."

" It is gambling," said Tom Norrie; " gambling with your own life for the stake and the world against you."

They were both quiet for some minutes after this. Tom thought perhaps the outlaw was considering the situation seriously at last, but when he finally broke the silence it was with a wholly irrelevant question.

" By the way, you didn't show me the picture of your girl the other day. I was just goin' to ask you for it when—well—we began talkin' about Jerroray and I forgot it, to tell the plain truth. Do you mind lettin' me look at her? "

" No, indeed," said Tom, producing the picture.

" She is a good-lookin' girl," exclaimed the outlaw. " Fine color, I suppose? "

" Yes," said Tom, " she has a good deal of color."

" Tall, too? "

" Yes—how did you know? "

" She looks it—a girl so spirited as that ought to be tall, sure. I like her looks a lot. She's worth fightin' for, and I shouldn't think you'd ever get licked while you had her to think about."

" It does make a difference," admitted Tom. " If I was licked I'd hate her to know it, and somehow that puts staying power into you, and makes you win in the end, even if you are overmatched."

CHAPTER XII

THE PROOF OF COURAGE

Three or four days after this, Snide, Trilby, and Button mounted their horses in the morning and rode away. Tom's suspicions were quickly aroused, and he was not surprised when Tom Nelson suggested to him later that he should get himself ready for a trip.

" Is it positively your last appearance in the rôle of train robber ? " he asked. Nelson nodded. " Just let me have your guns, please," he said.

" My pistols ? What for ? " asked Tom, alarmed.

" You're to go with us as a prisoner—not as an accomplice," exclaimed Mr. Nelson. " Then if you should be caught, bein' unarmed would be so much in your favor. It simply relieves you of all responsibility and you can enjoy yourself with a free heart— see ? "

Tom saw, but nevertheless felt uncomfortable with no means of defence, and wished he had kept his pistols.

They set out late in the afternoon, and riding slowly but steadily for four or five hours, made a halt finally in a curious sort of bowl dropped down between the rolling hills of the prairie, where the horses of the other three men awaited them with glad whinnies of greeting. The flat bottom of the place was some twenty feet in diameter, while the rise of ground about it was hardly higher than its width. On three sides it was precipitously steep, but in the fourth direction there was a gradual slope, down which they rode. They picketed their horses, rubbed them down and fed them, Tom doing what he saw the others do. The night was clear, but moonless and dark. They worked by the light of a single small lantern, hung up on a short stake in the centre of the bowl, and around this feeble luminary, when the horses were attended to, they took their hurried meal, which Gully had brought in a knapsack. Each man had a stiff drink of whiskey to put heart into him, as Nelson expressed it, though Tom noticed that as usual he took none himself.

" The thing itself is stimulus enough to
me," he said in an undertone, answering
Tom's thought.

Before they left the place the saddles and
bridles were put on all the horses again,
though some of them had not yet finished
their feed.

" We may be in a hurry when we come
back," said the outlaw, significantly. " Besides the bits will keep 'em from eatin' too
fast and gettin' indigestion."

They climbed up the sides of the bowl and
walked along for three or four minutes, Tom
taking observations of the stars to aid him
in keeping the direction back to the horses.
He stayed by Nelson's side, in hopes of having the plan of action more or less explained
to him, but the leader of the gang was
thoughtful and distraught, and nothing was
said until they reached the railroad track.
The dark prairie stretched away on every
side, crossed by this ribbon of track, which
was the only sign of human occupation.
There were no lights anywhere below to
answer to those above in the deep blue dome
of the sky. In the veiling shadows all the
unevennesses of the plain were lost, and it
seemed as flat as a great floor.

15

Tom's heart began to beat with the sense of mystery and excitement that grew upon him in the silent waiting. He thought of the train speeding toward them, miles away, along this iron track, and it seemed for the moment impossible, unreal, that he should be there with a band of desperate men ready to waylay it. Then it became terribly real, and he shuddered involuntarily at the thought of the deed he was about to witness, even though he took no part in it.

" Sorry you came ? " asked Nelson at his elbow. " You can't go back now, you know."

" I don't want to go back," said Tom, stoutly, " though I will confess that just at present train robbing doesn't seem to me so amusing a pursuit as it did."

" You ought to thank me, then, for takin' away your shootin' irons."

" I do, indeed," said Tom. " It's well enough to look on—but I'm pretty glad on the whole I'm not to bear a hand in it."

" Piety in your blood," observed the outlaw, cheerfully. " I had some in mine, too, to start with—but I got rid of it handily. The train's due in about ten minutes," he added, after a little, looking at his watch.

"You'll stay outside, of course. Remember you're a prisoner, and under Jinks's charge. If you try to make off he'll be likely to shoot you."

"Well, I sha'n't try," said Tom. "But aren't there any signals I ought to know or anything?"

"The danger signal is three rapid pistol shots."

"But I've no pistol."

. "Three anything then—three yells, three whistles, three stones through a car window. But we've never had to use a danger signal yet, and, besides, if you used it you'd be aidin' and abettin' us."

"That's my lookout. If the odious Trilby were to give you away, I'd be the first to want to aid and abet you."

"Trilby's not so bad as you think."

"He's a thief without honor," declared Tom Norrie, "and when it suits his convenience to go back on you he'll do it."

"Do you see the headlight?" asked Nelson, suddenly. "Look sharp, boys!"

He and Gully took their places, one on each side of the track, while Jinks turned on the lantern, which he had brought from the bowl, and gave a signal to the approaching

train, which he repeated at rapid intervals.
Tom, standing close beside him, saw that he
now wore a black mask, and looking quickly
towards the other two distinguished the same
sinister disguise, as they were shown up from
moment to moment by the small light in the
midst of the great darkness.   It seemed hours
to him before the train could be heard, and
hours again before the first distant rumble
grew into the immense engulfing roar which
bore down upon them, filling their ears and
seeming to annihilate them.   And those
hours, which were in truth but a few brief
moments, showed him how closely excitement is akin to fear.   He trembled violently,
and his heart beat so quickly and so fast that
it almost suffocated him ; he felt that he
could hear its beating even above the great
brazen clamor of the locomotive, as it drew
up and stopped, with a heavy jar, just beyond him, and stood there panting and
steaming like a live creature, its great heart
throbbing like his own.

Then in another instant this suffocating
excitement, which had been so like terror
that he felt a mere motion on the part of
one of the others would make him stampede
in an uncontrollable panic, left him com-

pletely.   His mind became clear and alert,
and he saw everything that happened.   Snide
had the engineer and fireman under full control.   Button appeared to be in possession
of the express car, and Trilby followed the
conductor out of the smoker and stood on
the platform with him as the train drew up.
A moment later he had both revolvers
drawn, one held at the conductor's head and
the other pointed down the length of the car.
This seemed to indicate a clear field to the
outlaw and his gang.   Gully leaped into the
express car, while Nelson, followed by Trilby,
went through the smoker.

Jinks moved on down the train on the outside, with a revolver in each hand, firing
shots in at the windows and doors, killing no
one, but effectually scaring everybody.   He
kept Tom with him, driving him under the
cars, or up over the platforms ahead of him,
as he crossed from side to side, emphasizing
all his orders with a very reckless and alarm-
ing use of his firearms.   The train was a
long one.   Tom became conscious suddenly
of movements at the farther end.   Beyond
the brightly lighted passenger coaches there
was a dark, shadowy mass like a freight car.

" Jinks," he said, suddenly, " there's a

horse down there, coming out of that last car."

Jinks swore a great oath of disbelief, but a moment later was convinced. "By God! the sheriff and his posse!" he cried out, and let off three quick shots from his revolver. "For the horses," he said to Tom, "and each man for himself. He rushed to tell Snide what had happened, and then struck out across the prairie, while Tom lingered a moment to watch Snide ordering the engineer and fireman to start up the locomotive, with threats of blowing their brains out if they refused. He saw Button leap out of one of the cars, and then in another moment Nelson, farther down, and staying for no more, put off like them at top speed for the horses. He fell twice at full length, and when he reached the bowl went headlong down the steep side, and was set on his feet by Jinks, who, reaching the place first, had unpicketed most of the horses. The four of them were mounted in a moment."

"You three ride along," said Nelson. "Keep together and get out of the way as fast as you can. I'll wait for the others."

The other two made off without more

ado, but Tom remained.   "I'd rather stay
with you," he explained.

"All right," said the outlaw.   "Keep
quiet."   There were sounds above, and then
Gully's voice was distinguished in muttered
oaths as he slid down the incline.

"Snide and Bub behind you?" asked
Nelson.

"Reckon so," said Gully, bestriding his
horse, "and a lot of men and horses,
too!"

"They'll not find us in here—or if they
do they'll break their necks," said Nelson.
"You'd better be off.   I'll wait a bit longer.
The boys'll have a close squeak of it if they
don't hurry."

Gully was off, and Snide appeared at the
same moment.   Snide had seen nothing of
Trilby, and, suggesting that he might have
gone back on them, advised leaving his
horse picketed in the bowl and saving their
own skins while there was yet time.   Nelson
agreed to this plan as the sound of many
galloping feet drew nearer and nearer, and
then the three set off at full speed, with
eight or ten horses in close pursuit behind.
They rode abreast in silence, while Tom
realized that Nelson, whose mare could easily

distance the others, was holding her in to keep with them.

"Their horses are d——d fresh," said Snide. "They'll gain on us soon, if they ain't already."

"Then we'll all go to jail together," replied Nelson, cheerfully.

His good faith throughout, and this undaunted spirit appealed to Tom powerfully. He was fond of him, too—he couldn't bear the thought of his being caught and sent to prison. An idea came to him, and hardly weighing it, he gave it quick utterance.

"You two ride on," he said "I'll change my course a little, keeping around to the left, and ride gradually slower and slower, but lead them as pretty a chase as I can. If I can get away I will, but if I can't it will only mean a short season of trouble for me, while for you it might be twenty years' hard labor."

Nelson demurred strongly at first, but Tom was in love with the idea and urged it warmly. "You've done me a good turn, now let me do you one. It costs me only a few days of confinement, or weeks at the most, and it will all be more or less fun for me. Come, there's no time to lose."

"He's a peach," declared Snide. "Let's give him his way, Cap—he's got the sense of it."

The outlaw yielded. "You're a good sort," he said. "And mind, tell them the straight story if they catch you, without trying to shield me—or Jack Potts. It's the only way. And then trust in me to the bitter end, for however sure they may be that you're Tom Nelson, I'll never let you go to prison in my place. Don't forget that."

"I'll not," said Tom. "Good-by."

Folly was off into the darkness like a shot, Snide's nag making a good second, while Tom's poor, faithful beast, already doing his utmost, was left quickly behind. He had good courage, however, and did not lose heart at the desertion of his comrades, but kept on resolutely.

"Good old fellow," said Tom. "You do the best you can, don't you?" He pulled the animal around all the time off the course of the other fugitives, though much against its will, and listening sharply behind could distinguish no division of forces in the pursuers. They were steadily gaining on him, and it was only a question of brief time when they should be up with him. But every minute was needed by those ahead, so Tom kept on, demanding all the speed his horse could give. Finally, when the men behind were near enough to send bullets whizzing about his ears, he reined in his horse and let them come up with him.

"Tricked, by hell!" exclaimed one voice.

"Where's the rest of the d——d crew?" said another.

They were all about him now, and one man threw the blinding rays of a dark lantern in his face. "Anyhow, it's the feller we wanted most," he cried out jubilantly, and Tom recognized the voice of the gallant Mr. Cutler Keach.

"Ah! Good-evening, Mr. Keach," he said, urbanely, holding out his hand. "I'm glad we're to have a chance to continue that little conversation of ours."

"Good-evenin', Mr. Nelson," responded Mr. Keach, somewhat taken aback. "But it's Marshal Goslin' that's wantin' the first hack at conversin' with you. And I'll wait until you get your handcuffs on before I shake hands with you, if you don't mind."

Tom easily turned the laugh that greeted

this sally, by observing that if it seemed more natural and homelike to Mr. Keach under such circumstances, he was quite will-ing.

Then in his surprise at being taken by anyone but the sheriff, he inquired for Mr. Roray, and learned that that gentleman having been out of town on business, the city marshal of Aurora had jumped at the chance to earn distinction for himself by capturing the notorious gang of train rob-bers in his absence.

" The Terror'll feel awful bad when he gets back," said his informant. " I know he wouldn't 'a' missed this scrap for nothin'."

The marshal, meanwhile, very much set up in his own importance at having done it all without the sheriff, was holding a con-sultation with his lieutenants, the upshot of which seemed to be that it was too dark a night to push on after the rest of the gang, gone now beyond sight and sound.

" You're sure this is Nelson himself? " he asked of Mr. Keach, who appeared to be his chief adviser.

" Let me make you 'quainted with Mr. Nelson, Mr. Goslin'," said Mr. Keach, with mock ceremony. " What could be a more agreeable task than to introduce a train robber to the happy man what's caught him ? ''

" Well, if you're Tom Nelson I'm d——d glad to meet you," said Mr. Gosling.

" I'm not Tom Nelson, unfortunately," said Tom Norrie, " but I'm none the less pleased to meet you on that account."

" Ho ! '' said Mr. Keach, contemptuously. " Goin' to try to prove an alibi, are you ? Caught red-handed, and set up ' it ain't me ' for a defence ! ''

" Well, Nelson or not Nelson, he's all we've got," said the marshal, " and we'd better be a-gettin' off home. Catchin' him's our business. We ain't the ones to decide who he is."

Tom's hands and feet were securely tied, and then, while one man led his jaded nag, three others surrounded him as a body guard. In this way the long and painful ride was accomplished, so wearisome to the already weary captive that he was glad indeed to see his prison at last, just as the first faint streaks of dawn began to lighten the blackness of the night.

" See here, Mr. Keach," he said as the

ropes were cut and he was allowed to dismount. "I'm not greatly stuck on this nag, but he's a good old soul, and he'll be pretty well done after this. Would you take him along and have your brother look after him? I'll see he's paid for his trouble."

Mr. Keach, with a thrifty eye to business, agreed at once, if he had the marshal's permission, and as Mr. Gosling was both sleepy and complaisant after the success of his exploit, the transaction was speedily arranged. Tom stipulated among other things that the poor Plunger should have a bed to his knees, and slept the better himself on the hard couch provided him by the State, for the consciousness that the tired horse was well cared for.

Tom Norrie, in the excitement of the moment, keenly touched by the outlaw's bravery and his faithfulness to his friends, had felt that he was undertaking but a small sacrifice on his behalf. The next day, or rather only five hours later the same day, when he was ruthlessly waked up to be taken before the justice of the peace, and incidentally before the whole town, assembled to a man in the court-house, and when no

one, during the ceremonies that followed,
would believe a word he said on any subject, and least of all his reiterated statement,
and, as he thought, proof, that he was not
Tom Nelson, the situation began to look to
him a little more serious. He was not required to say anything, being informed so
officially by the justice, and advised pri-
vately by the friendly sheriff, Aurora's celebrated Terror, in whose charge he now
found himself, to keep his mouth shut
until he'd seen his lawyer. But he had
notions of his own on the subject, and preferred to tell his story fully. With a feeling half of mistrust, half of contempt for the
law, derived from several generations of
Quaker ancestry, he had made up his mind
to conduct his case himself, with no aid
from the legal profession. Telling the
truth, the plain and entire truth, seemed to
him all that was necessary, and it was surely ridiculous to get a lawyer to help one do
that. But, to his surprise and grief, this
course of simple honesty was not attended
with the conspicuous success that he had an-
ticipated. He was not immediately set
free, nor did the justice professionally un-
bend, and congratulate him upon that noble

candor which was more powerful than any legal guile to unlock the doors of his prison.

On the contrary, while all the spectators were laughing, the justice preserved his own dignity with some difficulty, and the legal gentlemen present did not undertake to conceal how greatly entertained they were by Mr. Nelson's tale of adventures.

"D——d ingenious cuss," said the prosecuting officer, in an audible aside to one of the standers-by. " Say, wouldn't that yarn take in a dime novel? Trilby wouldn't be in it."

The part of his narrative which seemed specially to charm every one was the bold attempt throughout to cast suspicion upon the innocent Mr. Potts.

" Why, Jack Potts, he's been to the Palace Hotel off and on two or three months," said J. Cutler Keach, when he was at liberty to speak his mind to the prisoner after the examination, and while the officers in charge of him were awaiting the orders of the sheriff. " He's a mere lamb, he is, that never lifted his finger to harm nobody. There warn't any feller so hot on your trail as he was, and he thought you was a villain of the deepest dye. Guess he'd think so

more'n ever now if he could hear the way
you're a-layin' mud over him.''

Here, in exasperation, Tom committed a
grave fault in tact.   '' Jack Potts is a longer
headed gentleman than you ever dreamed
of,'' he said to Mr. Keach, a little contemptuously.   '' Can't you see that that was
his cue ?—that he was trying to wind you up
in your own conceit of your detective ability, and was laughing at you in his sleeve
all the time ? ''

'' Maybe I can see that—and maybe I can
see what you're a-drivin' at, too,'' said Mr.
Keach, with a large and catholic wink which
embraced all present.   '' As for Mr. Potts
he can tell his own story on the witness-
stand.''

'' A great lot you'll ever get him on any
witness-stand,'' said Tom, scornfully.

'' Just you wait and see,'' retorted Mr.
Keach.

'' He won't have to wait long either,''
said Charley Shore.   '' Court sits on Monday, and the Grand Jury'll go to work on
him right off.''

'' Yes,'' said Mr. Keach, with a satisfied
air.   '' Justice certainly is a-goin' to hustle
for once.''

Returned under close guard to the jail, bewildered by his inability to persuade his accusers to believe the simple truth, and with a sense of helplessness and anxiety which he could not shake off, it was an inexpressible relief to Tom Norrie to behold once more the friendly face of Jerroray. She was standing in the front door of the jail, a resplendent vision of flowered silk and white lace, with a gauzy hat and a gauzy parasol, a " corsij bokay " and a beaming smile, and Tom's heart warmed to her more than ever.

" Say—you're in a real bad fix, ain't you ? Well, I've got a pull, my dad bein' sheriff, and I've come to sweeten your captivity, like the girls do in stories. Now you men can just hand him over to me," she announced to the officers. " The Terror's given you his orders, and what he says goes. I'm to be jailer whenever I like. I've promised Terence I won't let the prisoner get away, and he knows my word's as good as his own. We're goin' to have Mrs. Jenks's sittin' room, and you can sit around and watch in the entry and under all the windows if you want to, though there ain't no need of it.   Mr. Chance is a gentleman, and he ain't agoin' to get a lady into trouble

16

by tryin' to light out when he's under her charge—are you, Chance?''

Tom gave his word emphatically that he should make no attempt whatever to get away, both for Miss Roray's sake and his own, for, being innocent, he wished to prove it in open court. And upon this declaration, supplementing her own previous ideas of his integrity of character, Jerroray, as her first act of authority, ordered his handcuffs taken off.

The snug, cosey room of Mrs. Jenks was a prison - cell to be dreamed of rather than realized, and Tom passed there the greater part of the next few days in the most agreeable custody that ever fell to the lot of captive man. The energetic friendliness of his jailer permitted no obstacle in the way of the completest comfort possible within his prison bounds. His bag and belongings arrived at once from the Palace Hotel, by the hand of G. Washington Keach. His own honeydew restored to him, the rubber pouch of which in his pocket had long been sadly empty, Tom was at once a happier and more placid man. With the full permission of the gracious lady, and cheered by her genial converse and informal manners, he smoked the long June hours away. Roses were in bloom beneath the windows, the sun shone and the birds sang, and Jerroray was no less entertaining than she was good to look at.

When they were comfortably settled that first afternoon, quite to the young lady's liking ; after she had watched Tom eat a good dinner—a much better dinner than he would have got had she not interceded with Mrs. Jenks before his return from the court-house; when with a satisfaction no less than his own, she had seen him light his pipe, and then made him lie down on Mrs. Jenks's carpet-covered lounge, while she put all the pillows she could find in behind him to soften the acerbities of that piece of furniture— she announced that she had a few remarks to make.

" 'Tell me that I'm to die to-morrow, if you like," said Tom, in blissful accents. " I'm so comfortable that I don't care what happens to-morrow."

" I do love to see folks comfortable," said Jerroray.

" And you certainly know how to make them so."

" It's the way I do to Terence when he's fagged. An' when I've got him all tucked away on a sofy—like you—then I fill his pipe and light it, and mix him a whiskey-toddy, and I can tell you he just purrs like a cat.''

'' I should think he would,'' said Tom, in an injured tone. '' You didn't mix me any toddy.''

'' Well, I will if you want me to ; I can do 'em awful good. I had a gentleman-friend once was a bar-keep, and he taught me lots of things. And then the sheriff himself ain't any slouch on mixin' drinks. Guess he could give points to some perfessionals.''

The whiskey-toddy proved to be a very choice mixture indeed, and if strong and a great lot of it, Tom reflected that at least he could spend the afternoon on its consumption. '' You didn't make any for yourself,'' he observed. '' I'll divvy with you.''

'' No, thanks, I don't indulge. I'm willin' other folks should fuddle their brains with the stuff, but I don't want any in mine—especially now when I propose to give my great head to your case.''

'' Will you be counsel for the defence ? '' asked Tom, with a laugh. I'm sure you'd get me off.''

" Well, if you want my advice, Chance, you've got to tell me the facts—all of 'em. That's what I had to say to you. It ain't pryin' curiosity, and you're at liberty not to bleat a word, an' we'll just talk about other things. But if we're goin' to discuss your situation at all, and try to get you out of your mux, then you've just got to sail in an' tell me the whole biz—the truth and nothin' but the truth. That's all. You can take your choice. An' you needn't be afraid I'll get mad if you don't tell me."

" But I want to tell you—I'd rather tell you."

" Well, now, that's bang-up—that's what I like," declared the young lady with great satisfaction. " To begin with then, what is your name really ? "

" It's to be a cross-examination, is it ? " said Tom. " Why should you think Chance isn't my name ? Do you, too, imagine I'm Tom Nelson ? "

" Potts said you warn't—and he talked like he meant it."

" Oh, he told you that, did he ? Well, I can guess why—it served his purpose."

" What do you mean ? "

" He didn't want you to think me Tom

Nelson for fear that would make you like me better than you did him.''

'' Oh !——But you ain't Tom Nelson, I'm 'most sure.''

'' I wish the other people were as sure,'' said Tom. '' Our astute friend, Mr. Potts, played his cards so well that they'll none of them hear a word against him.''

'' Against him—you don't mean——''

Tom watched with enjoyment the light beginning to dawn on Jerroray's face. '' Yes, I do,'' he said. '' Hadn't you guessed ? You're as stupid as I was.''

'' Oh, my ! '' she said, with wonder, awe, ecstasy, love, admiration and pride commingled in that very expressive ejaculation ; and '' Oh, my ! '' she repeated after a moment, as if no other form of speech could at all convey her many and overwhelming emotions.

'' You seem to like the idea,'' said Tom.

'' Like it ! '' she exclaimed, with an indescribable wriggle and shake of her whole person in the endeavor to express how much she liked it. '' Say, didn't I tell you he was great ? Didn't I say he was a peach ? My ! He's just out o' sight ! ''

'' You don't ask for any proof—it seems

very easy for you to believe that he's Tom Nelson."

"Course it is—it's exactly like him. I only wonder I didn't know it the minute I laid eyes on him. Say, have you seen him since the day you was up to our house?"

"I've spent the whole week with him."

"Oh, my !——Well, now just you tell me all about him, every word he said and everything he did."

"But you're forgetting all about my case. I was a fool not to pretend I was Tom Nelson myself."

"Well, you couldn't have worked the racket anyhow, if you'd a-tried. And I'm just as much interested in your case as ever —only any infant could see that the straight way out of it is through Nelson. So, just you tell me all about him."

Thus adjured, Tom told the tale from beginning to end, not even omitting what Nelson had said about retiring from his present business, and adopting one more compatible with matrimony. "But of course you'd never marry a train-robber," he observed, carelessly.

"Wouldn't I? Just you wait till I'm

asked! My! I'm so glad he's the one after all, and I can play him straight now."

Tom made inquiry as to the meaning of this naïve remark, and was greatly entertained with Jerroray's tale of her tantalizing doubts and uncertainties — now, however, resolved so entirely to her mind."

" So you really did like me a little? " he questioned.

" Course I did, and I always will. And you've behaved just grand about it all. Lots o' fellers wouldn't have told me a thing, but would just have humped for 'emselves without ever thinkin' of my feelin's or Nelson's. But you've been just as square as a feller could be, and I'm your friend for life. Shake."

This ceremony performed, Tom continued his narrative up to the outlaw's final promise to stand by him whate'er befell, and get him out of any and every difficulty he might find himself in.

" He'll do it, too," said Jerroray. " That settles all my worries. We needn't take any trouble. He'll get you out of the ditch. We can just loaf and have as good a time as we like, and not fret ourselves."

When Tom told her finally, however, of

his examination of the morning, and the anxieties which had harassed him since, she made up her mind at once that he must have as good a lawyer as could be procured.

" Of course, you've got to have a lawyer," she said. " 'Tain't so much a question of tellin' lies or tellin' the truth, as how you do whichever you do do. Lawyers know how, and that's what you pay 'em for. We want a good one, and we want him right off. I'll go and find out who's the best man can be got down to Bloomer—though I'll bet in advance they'll all say Bob Trout. He's a daisy lawyer, he is, and I just admire to hear him argue a case. If I was a jury I couldn't ever help findin' for him."

She consulted with her father, and with the prosecuting attorney, set down what they said about different legal lights, and brought these data to Tom for consultation.

Their choice, Colonel " Bob " Trout, as Jerroray had predicted, and one of the best-known criminal lawyers in the State, arrived the next day. He was tall, with a hawk nose and piercing black eyes ; he wore a very long-tailed frock coat and a silk hat ; but as the hat was perched on the back of his head and the coat never buttoned up, he

failed of the elegance he aspired to. He
knew all about the train robberies, and took
it for granted from the start that Tom was
the man who had committed them. When
Tom finished his truthful tale of the ways
and means by which he had been brought to
his present pass, Colonel Trout said, briefly :

" Excellent story—do very well in the
main for our defence, with some few altera-
tions. Now tell me the exact facts. I never take a case unless my client tells me the
truth."

In spite of Tom's protest that this was
what he had just done, and his stoutness
in holding to his story through the violent
cross-examination he was at once put to,
Colonel Trout seemed never quite to abandon his belief in his client's guilt. This had
a depressing effect upon Tom in their constant association before the trial. He re-
sented the little traps his counsel laid to catch
him, springing on him every now and then a
sharp and sudden question, designed to take
him unawares and make him betray himself.

And when the colonel learned of what he
called Tom's crazy folly in telling his whole
story without one reserve to the justice of
the peace, he became, in his grief and rage,

even more unpleasant to his client. His feelings were almost too much for words, he explained, by way of logical excuse for his violent language, and Tom could not help retorting that it would have been better if they had been quite too much.

"There's no use talking about it," he said, " the thing's done, and I'm not sorry. It seems to me we'd better devote ourselves to making the best of the situation as it is."

The chief necessity of the defence, of course, was to prove alibis for Tom on the dates of the first four train robberies. He had been in the outlaw's camp at the time of the fifth, and had admitted beyond recall his presence at the sixth and last. But if they could prove that he was in Lincoln, Nebraska, when the first one occurred, down in Beaver County at the time of the second, at Titus City on the date of the third, and many miles from Bud, on the Red Gulch road, on the day of the fourth, arriving in Bud by train a full hour and a half after the hold-up, the case would be two-thirds won. Unluckily Tom had found no congenial companions on the Red Gulch train, and it was an even chance that no one would remember him well enough to be safe on cross-examination.

Moreover, on laboriously counting back, he was not himself certain whether he had left Lincoln on the 6th or 7th of May, and he had stayed there with a very doubtful travelling companion, at a hotel which was practically a gambling joint of the worst description ; so that even if willing " friends " could be found to testify to his having been there on the important date, they would not be gentlemen calculated to make a good impression on a jury.   On neither of the other dates could he do much better, for he had not been at hotels, and there would be neither the registers, nor witnesses to testify to payments of money, to give an air of authority to the evidence.   At the earlier time he was staying at the country seat of a gentleman of bibulous and poker-playing proclivities known to his friends as " Tank." Mr. Tank Fergusson had since, it seemed, gone to prison on a charge of aggravated assault, having accidentally shot another gentleman, on an hilarious occasion when he was " not himself," and was genially winding up a pleasant evening by shooting in at people's windows in a random and childlike manner. But though he was somebody else while he was drunk and did the shooting, he had to go to prison nevertheless in his own person, and pay the penalty of too marked a taste for masquerading.

The later date was that of the shooting match at Titus City, and as Tom had distinguished himself by standing second in the score, there might be found various gentlemen, less fortunate, who would remember the tenderfoot who beat them. His particular chum on that day had been a rover and soldier of fortune like himself. They had come into Titus City by train, very early in the morning after a long, hot journey, sleeping in a common car ; and had left it twenty-four hours later by the same train, having made a night of it in celebration of the match. The chances were nine to ten that Billy Buck, or Bucking Billy, as he preferred to be called, could not now be found to testify in favor of his pal pro tem. He had talked of Tacoma and also of Phœnix as places he yearned to visit, and he might equally well be in Boston or New Orleans.

The outlook was dark indeed, but the colonel, having brought up the money question, received a good-sized retaining fee, and satisfied himself that he was safe on the rest from a client of business connections so dis-

tinguished as our hero's, despatched his
emissaries and telegrams in every direction ;
while Tom, relying on the outlaw far more
than on the law, and enjoying daily the vivacious conversation of Jerroray, did not
greatly trouble himself.

The Grand Jury, sitting on Monday at
the opening of Rising Sun's spring term of
court, found a true bill against the prisoner
for conspiring with John Doe and Richard
Roe and other evil-disposed persons to commit this series of train robberies against the
peace and dignity of the State, and especially of Rising Sun County.

The prisoner was arraigned in court and
pleaded not guilty.   The Judge then suggested that in view of the enormity of the
offences, their unusual extent, the expense
to the State of delay, and the desire of the
public for a speedy trial, it should occur as
soon as possible.   With the consent both of
the prosecuting officer and of Colonel Trout,
the time was set for the following Thursday.
The Judge placed the bail at $10,000, but
Tom, very comfortable in jail and confident
of a speedy release, did not take the trouble
to procure it.

CHAPTER XIII

On the morning of the trial the town bore the aspect of a Fair Day, or the Fourth of July. All Rising Sun and Creosote Counties were there. They came with their entire families, and brought with them copious supplies of food for themselves and their live stock. Some arrived the night before, but most of them poured into the town that morning, on foot, on horseback, in carts, on bicycles, or by the trains. The nearest mining camps sent large contingents, and there was even a crowd from Bloomer, with flashily dressed women and sporty looking men. Everyone wanted to see Tom Nelson, the celebrated outlaw. Though the court-house could not contain one-tenth part of the people who crowded without it, they did not cease to crowd, each one determined, for his own part, to get in. The doors were opened at half-past eight, and two minutes

later the room was full, terribly, insuffera-
bly full, with disappointed hundreds still
scrambling without. These had, however,
a measure of compensation. The happy
thought came to them to go up to the jail,
a quarter of a mile away, and await the prisoner. Here they aroused great consterna-
tion. There were so many of them, and
they were so boisterous and noisy, that the
authorities were alarmed. The mayor was
sent for, and began to read them the riot
act from the roof of the porch, when the
crowd set up a great howl of amusement.

"Oh, shut up your guff!" they cried.
"We don't want no riot act. We ain't
makin' no row. All we want is Nelson."

Then they began to shout the prisoner's
name, with yells, cat-calls, cheers, and other
demonstrations which effectively drowned
the mayor's voice. Finding, however, that
they secured nothing by this method, they
finally selected a big miner for spokesman,
and he explained to the mayor and sheriff
that they meant no harm whatever to the
prisoner ; far, indeed, from havin' thoughts
of lynchin' him they'd be more inclined, if
anything, to set him free—he was such a
d——d smart feller, and they couldn't help

takin' pride in him as a product of their own region—they could beat the world on train robbers if on nothin' else. But they'd come now merely to escort him in honor to the court-house, and they'd solemnly promise not to interfere with the course of justice. Only if they didn't get a sight of Tom Nelson, and that pretty d——d quick, they'd not answer for any accidents that might occur.

Whereupon, with all speed, the prisoner was produced, attended by the mayor, the Terror, three or four deputies, and the entire police force of the city of Aurora—which last august body consisted of the marshal, Mr. Gosling, and three policemen. They all bore arms, and Tom, with his handcuffs on, moved in their midst. As he appeared upon the porch, smiling and undaunted— for he had heard the speech and knew that he had nothing to fear from a crowd so entirely in his favor—a great shout went up. Then the big miner proposed three cheers for Tom Nelson, and they were given with enthusiasm. Behind the miner, Tom caught sight of another big man, with clean shaven cheeks and chin, in bluish contrast to the deep bronze of the rest of his countenance. There was something familiar about him,

17

and Tom turned quickly to look for him
again, but he was lost in the sea of faces.
The crowd fell a little apart as the prisoner
and his escort moved down from the porch,
received them into its bosom, surrounded
and engulfed them, and bore them on irre-
sistibly, like the current of a great river.
The murmur of the many voices deepened
now and then to a louder roar, and again
grew less, as the waves of the sea crash upon
the sands, and draw back and crash again.

Borne along thus like a conqueror by the
surging movement of a great throng, of
whose movement he was the spring, and of
their thoughts the pivot, Tom felt a sense
of strong elation, a wish that he were indeed
Tom Nelson, a pride that at least he knew
the hero and had been his friend and com-
rade. This spontaneous outburst in his favor did not strike him as strange. Like all
success, it only increased his admiration for
the outlaw, and he longed to tell these men
around him, whose faces were so eagerly
scanning his face, that though he was not
the man they thought, yet he knew and liked
and admired him with all his heart.

Thus when they reached the court-house
and the crowd refused to let them enter until

Tom Nelson had made them a speech, Tom Norrie was at no loss.

" Let me speak—it's the only thing to quiet them, and will do no harm," he said to the attendant Terror at his side, who, with a drawn revolver, had not relaxed vigilance for a moment.

" All right, speak ahead, but don't blow yourself empty," returned that official, having satisfied himself that the Judge had not yet arrived.

And Tom, with admirable art, and an eloquence most unexpected to himself, said a great deal in very little, fanning the fire of Tom Nelson's large popularity and creating at the same time a small popularity of his own. " Let the law take its course," he wound up, " and if it goes wrong and I am sent to prison, your outlaw will then take his course. I trust to him and so must you. If instead of law and order to-day it turns out to be law and disorder, he will give the law a black eye." (Wild cheers.) " He knows I am innocent, and he is too brave a man, and too honest, to let another suffer in his place. They call him a thief, but if all men who are not thieves were as brave and as honest as he, the world would be a pleasanter place to live in. Now, gentlemen, this is all I have to say, and if you will give three cheers for Tom Nelson, I will go and stand my trial, trusting to you that all shall pass off peaceably.''

The three cheers for Tom Nelson were followed by three for the prisoner, ''whether he's Nelson or some other feller,'' as one man shouted ; and ''a plucky gent anyhow,'' declared a second.

The speech made the occasion seem more like a Fourth of July than ever, and had drawn the curious crowd out of the courthouse to listen to it. Now, as the prisoner was led into the building, a wild scramble took place again for seats, and a new crowd, comprising many of the so-called rioters, occupied the place.

The trial began promptly at nine o'clock. Not much difficulty was had in securing an unprejudiced jury, and then the case of the State against Thomas Norrie, Jr., alias J. Chance, alias Tom Nelson, was opened by Mr. William Warble, the attorney-general, who had come down especially from Boreal to grace the occasion with his prestige and importance, and render the conviction of the notorious train robber as certain as possi-

ble.   Colonel Trout had previously expressed
to Tom his abundant contempt for this gentleman, who had been but recently elevated
to his position, and owed it entirely to political services rather than to legal ability,
of which he had none.   And besides, the
merest justice demanded that Bloomer should
have had the attorney-generalship instead of
such a mere village as Boreal.

" Warble's a fat fool—a complacent, tow-
headed chump," said the colonel, superior
in the consciousness of his own tall, brunette
beauty.   " We're lucky that his conceit
brings him down here, for if it had been left
to the county prosecutor, he'd have made
something of the case.   Warble's so stuck on
himself that he needs a searchlight to see
anything else."

And in truth, in spite of the great dignity
of the attorney-general, and his very important manner, the case he outlined seemed to
Tom by no means a strong one.   It consisted chiefly in the facts that the prisoner
was caught on the night of the last hold-up,
not five miles from the scene thereof, riding
away in the dark on a rather slow horse,
while there was some evidence also to indicate that he had not been absent on the oc-

casions of the five earlier robberies. Mr.
Warble explained elaborately that the State
had no wish to convict an innocent man, and
if the prisoner were innocent, as he claimed,
he (Warble) should greatly prefer to see him
go free.   The State only wished to see justice
done, and the guilty alone punished for their
misdeeds.   He was there in the service of
the State to put the jury in the possession of
the plain, truthful facts of the case, as clearly
as was in his power ; and then from these
facts, kept ungarbled by the sophistry and
misrepresentations of the defence, the jury
were to decide whether the prisoner were
guilty or not guilty.   They knew well how
serious and awful a thing it was to send a
man—and a young man—to state-prison, and
they would not dream of doing it unless the
evidence were so strong against him as to
render any other course impossible—which,
however, the prosecution would shortly show
them to be the case.

" The defence will try to prove," said
Mr. Warble, " that the prisoner is really
Mr. Thomas Norrie, Jr., who disappeared
from his home in one of the great cities of
the Eastern seaboard, on the 25th of April,
1895, and has not been heard of since.

They may prove it or not prove it—it is
immaterial to us.   You will observe that the
date of his disappearance is just ten days before the first train robbery, and are aware
that we are not half that time distant from
New York.   The prisoner, when at home,
may be as many gentlemen, and as many
kinds of gentlemen as he pleases.   Our business is to find out whether he is Tom Nelson
or not, and if he is Tom Nelson he must
meet his just deserts, no matter how many
seemingly innocent persons he has been before or may contemplate being hereafter.
To show, in short, how little the State cares
about his name or record outside of her
boundaries he was named in the indictment
Thomas Norrie, Jr.''

As one of the chief points on which Tom's
counsel had relied for a successful defence
was the, to him, very impressive fact that
his client was a partner in the wealthy and
widely known manufacturing firm of Norrie,
Trumbull & Co., he was a little disconcert-
ed by Mr. Warble's willingness to admit it.
But this was the only thing in the address
which really disturbed the colonel at all.

Nor did the evidence at first seem particularly damaging, relating as it did entirely

to the last hold-up, as if Mr. Warble meant
that to be his chief point of attack.   The
earliest witnesses, most of them passengers
on the train that night, stated, one after another, that although they could not see the
robber's face for his mask, Tom resembled
him in every particular so far as they had
been able to see him, being of the same
height and build, having the same color of
hair, the same general look and manner of
a gentleman, and above all the same voice.
As each fresh witness was introduced a screen
was placed before Tom and five other men
who sat with him, and each man or woman
listening to the six voices behind the screen,
was required to identify that of the train
robber.   Colonel Trout objected violently
when this scheme was first proposed, badè
Tom not to speak a word, and proclaimed
loudly his inalienable right not to be compelled to incriminate himself.   Tom held a
brief, whispered consultation with his counsel, however, whereupon the colonel arose
all smiles and urbanity, and said that his
client was so confident that his innocence
would win the day in the end, that he was
willing to submit to that or any other test,
although perfectly aware, from his own

knowledge of the train robber, as would be brought out in the case for the defence, that their voices were surprisingly alike. Whereupon the witnesses for the prosecution, one by one pitched on Tom's voice the moment he spoke, with a unanimity which had a visible effect upon the jury, but which Colonel Trout later on gallantly attempted to turn into evidence favorable to the defence.

But if the case for the prosecution in the hands of Mr. Warble began like a modest and unimportant brook, it swelled through the morning into a great and mighty river. Little bit by little bit Tom's spirits ebbed before the great array of evidence prepared by the county prosecutor and brought in by the attorney-general, to prove the seemingly modest propositions of his address. Things that he had quite forgotten or overlooked, mere accidents of ill-luck, were brought up and piled on the great total of circumstantial evidence, until as the hours went by the prisoner saw that the case of the State against him was one that could scarcely be broken. From the sixth train robbery the attorney-general went back to the others, and brought out rapidly, by means of many witnesses, the story of the first four. Every witness who

had been in a hold-up testified to the prisoner's striking resemblance in voice and general appearance to the train robber.

His arrival in Bud on the evening of the
fourth hold-up was certified to by Mr. Augustus B. Dicker, clerk and bar-tender of
the Empire Hotel at Bud; Mr. Job Swinney and others, habitués of that hostelry;
and Mr. Edward P. Bedloe, Mr. Charles S.
Shore, and other gentlemen from Aurora,
temporarily staying there on the occasion
of Bud's great ball. It was shown that the
hold-up occurred some time after dark, about
a mile and a half outside of Bud, and that
the prisoner, giving his name as Chance,
and his residence as " Burr Oak, Nebraska,"
had turned up at the Empire Hotel a couple
of hours or so later, within fifteen minutes
of the arrival of the evening train on the
Red Gulch Road, by which he stated that
he had come. Every one had noticed from
the first that he was a suspicious-looking in-
dividual. He had evinced an enormous interest in Tom Nelson and all his perform-
ances, and would in fact talk of little or
nothing else, though he professed that he had
never even heard of the train robberies
before that night.

Mr. Swinney, whose voluble tongue re-
tailed these latter facts before Colonel Trout
could stop him, was anxious to tell also all
his suspicions about Mr. Chance, and all his
other thoughts and emotions before or since,
but was finally suppressed by Colonel Trout's
animated objections.

The chambermaid of the Empire Hotel reported that she had thought Mr. Chance a
little out of the ordinary, and had hence in-
vestigated the contents of his valise, and observed with interest all the pretty red T.
N.'s on his underclothing and the white ones
on his handkerchiefs. She, too, went on
talking, and her course could not be arrested until she had brought out, to the delight of the crowd, the interesting and suspicious fact that, instead of sleeping in the
usual nightshirt, or even the underwear he
had worn by day, Mr. Chance went to bed
in a coat and trousers of thin pink and white
silk, fastened by a sort of small frog—"awful pretty," said the chambermaid—"nice
enough for a bride."

Mr. Warble pointed out later to the jury
the effete luxury and depravity indicated
by such unmanly, such essentially feminine,
nocturnal apparel as this. "What could

you expect of such a man but that he would
be a low criminal and a highway robber?"
he inquired, indignantly. "The British
aristocracy, gentlemen, those shameless dukes
and earls with whose shocking ways of cor-
ruption and sin you are doubtless all familiar, probably wear these befrilled and fur-
belowed costumes every night of their lives.
If we are to keep our own great country in
its present pure and unspotted innocence we
must not tolerate these hateful foreign customs—we must exterminate them, gentlemen, root and branch; that is to say, coat
and pants, and cling to the simplicity of the
republican nightshirt. The great Nordau
himself would surely agree with me that such
garments as these are but another sign of that
Fin der Sickle degeneracy that leads inevitably to common thieving, gentlemen—I repeat it, common thieving."

Colonel Trout, in his own speech, retorted
upon Mr. Warble here with crushing scorn.
These articles of wearing apparel, which that
distinguished gentleman had apparently never
heard of before, were just ordinary pajamas,
made and worn in America in large quantities, and no more foreign than Plymouth
Rock pants. If the dukes and earls wore
them, so also did Mr. Chamberlain and Mr.

Gladstone, and, nearer at home, such great
men as President Cleveland and ex-President
Harrison, even T. B. Reed and Major Mc-
Kinley, and probably all the other Presidential candidates of 1896—in short, the Four
Hundred everywhere, but train robbers nowhere. The singular ignorance of society
customs in the mind of the eminent counsel
for the prosecution indicated his lifelong
residence in the backwoods hamlet of Boreal.
Pajamas in Bloomer were as thick as peas,
and in short there was no better argument
in favor of Mr. Norrie's entire innocence
than the fact that he wore these highly cultivated and even reserved—yes reserved—
garments. Colonel Trout had the honor to
belong to the Browning Society of Bloomer,
a club in which were represented all the
wealth and fashion of that eminently modern city, and at the next meeting he should
himself take occasion to suggest that all its
members who had not already done so should
at once adopt the wearing of pink and white
silk pajamas, as a badge, as it were, of cult-
ure, refinement, and style."

Mr. Warble declared hotly that he should
never give his vote for any Presidential
candidate who wore this lewd and foreign

night attire, and he hoped that all true Americans would follow his lead ; and as for Bloomer's Browning Society, like all other such societies throughout the length and breadth of the United States, the men were all chumps and the women all frumps.

But these little amenities did not occur till the final summing up, and in carrying the pajama episode through to the end we are moved only by a desire to clear out of the way all such distracting minor incidents, that the tragic march of the main events may move on undisturbed.

Tom Norrie's speeches and actions at the ball were brought out one by one with a fatal significance that appalled him. The evidence of the revengeful Mr. Charley Shore was particularly damaging, but Colonel Trout turned it neatly by his method of cross-examination.

Q. You were engaged to Miss Geraldine Roray up to the night of the fourth hold-up ?

A. (Sulkily.) " Yes."

Q. You quarrelled on the train in regard to Miss Roray's way of talking to the train robber ?

A. I suppose you'd say quarrel.

Q. Then she met the prisoner, Mr. Chance, at the ball?

A. Yes.

Q. And seemed much taken with him?

A. He was taken with her.

Q. She danced with him ten times?

A. I don't remember how many times.

Q. But she only danced with you once?

A. That's all.

Q. And, as we may say, gave you the mitten the next morning?

A. (Sulkily.) Yes.

Q. And it was not until she ceased to allow you to bask in the sunshine of her eyes that you began to suspect that Mr. Chance was the train robber, and to act on that suspicion?

A. (Hedging.) Well—

Q. Answer directly, Mr. Shore. Did it enter your head that the prisoner was the train robber before the lady bounced you? Yes or No.

A. No.

" That will do, that will do," said Colonel Trout. " That's all I want of you."

The other young men he cross-examined with similar tact and sharpness to their own discomfiture, to the delight of the audience,

and with some effect upon the jury. Mr.
Cutler Keach was, however, less tractable.
Both on examination and cross-examination
he made many strong points for the prosecution, and turned the laugh cleverly upon
Colonel Trout, though he was never able to
disturb that gentleman's coolness and ease.

Tom looked to Jerroray's evidence to correct, if anything could, all that was against
him, and turn the tide once more in his
favor.   Colonel Trout had been greatly surprised that with her well-known predilec-
tions she should be called as a witness for
the prosecution.

"Warble'll get left when he tackles her.
He don't know women," said the colonel,
with a superior air of knowing himself all
there was to know.

And Jerroray had just sent him a little
note by her faithful slave and father, the
sheriff.   "Warble's had his innings," she
wrote, "and his side's made a big score,
with lots of three-base hits and home runs,
I admit.   But we aren't beaten yet.   I'm
coming to the bat pretty quick myself, and
I'm onto the fat man's curves.   You can bet
I'm not going to fan the air."

Thinking of this encouraging prospect,

amused at the way the young lady had mixed the analogies of the national game and lawsuits in her mind, and with his eyes wandering aimlessly over the court - room, Tom caught sight suddenly of the same face he had noticed in the crowd before the jail. It was familiar, yet not familiar, and puzzled him, as he found it impossible to recall where or when he had seen it before. But just then a new witness was called, and he turned quickly to see Jerroray herself being escorted to the stand. She looked more brilliantly handsome than ever, in one of her most stunning costumes, with the widest white sailor-collar that could be imagined extending out over navy blue sleeves that were wider still. A murmur of admiration went through the crowded court-room, but she looked only at Tom, with a smile of friendliness and confident serenity.

Colonel Trout, unpleasantly surprised at his scorned rival's success thus far in the case, and, wishing, as he explained to Tom, to "rattle" him, remarked here in an undertone, quite audible to the jury, that it was a shame to call so innocent and lovely a young lady upon any witness-stand.

Mr. Warble, overhearing him as he intended, became heated and indignant at once, and retorted aloud that reluctant as he was to bring so estimable and superior a young woman into the case, he had been forced to it by the inconsiderate and ungentlemanly behavior of the prisoner, the client of his honorable friend.   This cowardly villain had so forced himself upon the society of Sheriff Roray's beautiful daughter, and entirely against the wishes of her discreet and maidenly modesty, that she unfortunately knew things which no other human being could tell them, and it was only on this account that he had reluctantly done his duty and called her to the service of the State.   No more entirely admirable young lady ever lived than Miss Geraldine Roray, and the dastardly manner in which her name had been dragged into the case by the unnatural blackguard——''

'' Come, come, Warble,'' interrupted Colonel Trout, sarcastically, '' this may be a good enough way to manage the cases before a justice that you've been accustomed to, but it ain't the way we try jury cases.''

And the Court, having listened up to this point with an impartial smile, now suggested to the attorney-general that he had said all

that was necessary to say, and might proceed with the examination of the witness.

"But before he starts up," remarked Jerroray, pleasantly, to the Judge, "I would
like to observe in my own behalf that Chance
is one of my most intimate gentlemen-friends
and not a villain, or a coward, or a blackguard, or any other of the names that General Warble just called him, and he never
forced himself on my society or dragged me
into this case, but I would have come into it
anyway of my own accord, for I would like
to prove, what I know to be true, that he's
no more a train robber than I am." She
got this off so quickly, raising her voice
louder and louder as Mr. Warble began to
object, that the Court hadn't time to stop
her, and the audience broke into cheers as
she finished.

"The next man that raises his voice in
this court-room will be instantly ejected,"
said the Judge severely when the noise subsided. "And witnesses that display contempt of court will be dealt with according
to their deserts."

"Oh, now, Judge, come off the bench,"
said Jerroray, with a grin. "You know I
didn't mean contempt of court, and you and

I are good chums anyhow, and I want to
work this racket to suit you just as near as
I can.   But it ain't fair, now you know it
ain't, to let Warble blacken the prisoner's
character, and if you let him do that you'll
have to let me stand up for him, else I'll
never mix you another toddy—and you know
you like my toddies.''

The crowd laughed irrepressibly at this,
and a genial smile overspread the august
countenance of the Court.

''That's very true, Geraldine,'' he said,
''and I also like your conversation.   It's
much more entertaining than that of our distinguished friend the attorney-general—but
suppose you give him a chance now?''

''All   right,''   said   Jerroray.   ''That's
square.   Fire away, General Warble.''

Mr. Warble looked as if he would like to
commit the whole court for contempt of Mr.
Warble.   His usually bland eye was flashing,
and he meant business when he began to
examine the sheriff's popular daughter.   He
had apparently been well primed by the vin-
dictive Charley Shore, and he knew exactly
what questions to ask.   He brought out at
once the facts that Jerroray was on the train
the night of the fourth hold-up, had been

obliged to part with all her jewelry, and had then gone on to the ball at Bud. Her conversation with the train robber was repeated in full, and with Mr. Warble's artful little touches would have indicated to any unprejudiced listener that Tom Nelson's fancy had been decidedly caught by Miss Geraldine Roray, and that his advice to her not to marry Mr. Shore might easily be construed to indicate that he had his eye on the succession. Mr. Warble pinned the young lady down to estimating exactly that it was above an hour and a half, but less than two hours, after the hold-up when the prisoner appeared in the ball-room and was immediately brought to be introduced to her. He made her repeat their conversation, Tom's expressions of admiration for the train robber, his condoning of the enormity of his crimes, his statement that he would like to join Mr. Nelson's gang, his wager that he would bring her back her diamonds.

" The prisoner reminded you strongly of the train robber? "

" No, he didn't," said Jerroray, defiantly, and Mr. Warble looked surprised and pained.

" Yet you said so later to several persons? "

"Well, that's straight, ain't it? When I said so he did, of course, but that ain't sayin' he did before, or does now."

"Ah, I see," observed Mr. Warble. "Perhaps it would be more correct to say that he struck you as familiar when you first saw him. Did he?"

"Oh, kind of."

"He paid you very marked attention during the evening?"

"Well, you've heard how mad it made Charley Shore and the other fellers, haven't you?" (General laugh.)

"And you constantly had this feeling of having seen him before somewhere?"

"I reckon so."

"How long was it until you decided that he reminded you of the train robber?"

"Next morning—Mr. Potts——"

"You have answered my question," said Mr. Warble, interrupting her quickly. "Now tell me if you were not very much struck with the resemblance as soon as you thought of it?"

"I don't know as you'd say very much struck," said Jerroray, indignant at not being allowed to say that Mr. Potts first suggested it to her.

" Come, come, Miss Roray. Were you not confident later that he was himself the train robber ? "

" Well, everybody else seemed to think so."

" And it seemed to you perfectly possible ? "

" Oh, of course, anything's possible."

" Answer the question directly. Were you not sure at one time that the prisoner was actually the train robber ? "

" Well, yes. But I didn't think so long —not more'n two or three hours—Jack Potts——"

" Confine your answers to the questions asked, if you please," said Mr. Warble, severely.

Then to Tom's great surprise and that of his counsel, the attorney-general brought out the part Jack Potts had played in his escape, how he had brought the horse, told the prisoner of his danger, started him off on the mare, stayed and talked ten minutes, then followed him on horseback and returned of course without him, while the sheriff and his posse were still reconnoitring about the Roray mansion. All the crushing facts about Jack Potts which they had hoped to elucidate on cross-examination Mr. Warble brought out as triumphantly as if they constituted his most important evidence ; then bowed politely to Colonel Trout and said, with the conscious flush of victory :

" The witness is in your hands."

Tom marvelled that the colonel, rising promptly to his feet, looked no less triumphant than the attorney-general.

" When the proper time comes," said Colonel Trout, " I shall have a great many questions to ask Miss Roray, as one of the chief witnesses for the defence. Now I shall be content with but two or three. Miss Roray, I want you to tell me who first suggested to you the idea that the prisoner resembled the train robber ? "

" Jack Potts," said Jerroray, promptly.

" Exactly," said the colonel, satisfied with the sensation produced by this statement. " And when was this ? "

" On the train, the day after the hold-up and the ball."

" And did the alleged Mr. Potts convey the same impression to other occupants of your car ? "

" I should just smile. He stirred every-

body all up about it, a-lookin' and a-smilin'
and just hintin' things.''

" That will do. That's all I want now,"
said the colonel.

Mr. Warble, however, rose to a fresh attack
with undiminished alacrity. " I should like
to introduce the evidence of Mr. Potts himself just here," he said, " but he cannot arrive till the noon train. We will proceed
to the fifth train robbery, which took place
three days after Mr. Nelson's escape from
Aurora. We will have the screen placed before Mr. Nelson—I beg pardon, Mr. Chance
—or should I say Mr. Norrie?" he said
with great politeness. " The screen, if you
please, as we desire each witness to identify
the prisoner first by his voice.''

Tom had grown accustomed to the monotony of the process, and amused himself
by noticing the way in which the witnesses
themselves spoke, and wondering if he could
identify them if he ever had a chance.
Three witnesses, two men and a woman,
picked him out unerringly by his speech and
told their tales. A fourth was brought in,
a woman with a cultivated voice at the
tones of which Tom Norrie's heart stood
still. It was a voice he could have iden-

tified anywhere, at the ends of the world, after a hundred years, a voice that for all his fancied attraction to the friendly and delightful Jerroray was the sweetest thing in the world to him, and would ever be. The witness had been in the last hold-up, she said, and had lost all her jewels, which she invariably kept with her in a small bag, and $200 in money. Tom's heart grew cold at the fatality of it. She had come all that way to convict him—her evidence would be fatal.

" You remember the robber's voice well ? " said Mr. Warble.

" Perfectly."

" Had you any special reason for noticing and remembering it ? "

" I had—it reminded me of the voice of a friend."

" You do not think it could have been your friend ? "

" Oh, no, indeed," with a little laugh. "That would be quite impossible. But the likeness was so marked that I am sure I should know his voice in a moment if I heard it again."

Tom sat at the beginning of a row of five. Mr. Warble held up four fingers, and the fourth man spoke the formula agreed on.

"That is not the voice," said the witness, in deep, serious tones that thrilled Tom through and through.

Mr. Warble held up three fingers and the third man spoke.

"No," said the witness; "that is not it."

Mr. Warble held up one finger, and with a heart beating like a trip-hammer Tom uttered the brief words.

The witness gave a cry. "That is it," she said. "I should know the voice anywhere."

"Now," said Mr. Warble, affably, "tell us which of the five men resembles most your memory of the train robber. Officer, remove the screen."

The officer removed the screen and Tom and Janet Trumbull found themselves face to face.

She gave one wild scream. "Oh, Tom—Tom!" she cried. "It isn't you—it can't be you!" and sank back on a chair, covering her face with her hands. Jerroray was sitting close by and sprang to her aid. A tremor of excitement went through the court-room. Tom was pale as death and trembling, and every one looked from her to him and from him to her.

Mr. Warble seemed no less surprised than every one else by what had happened, but as soon as Janet had somewhat recovered herself he resumed his examination. "You had known the prisoner before?" he asked.

"Yes," she answered, faintly.

"He was the friend you spoke of—of whose voice you were reminded by the train robber's?"

"Oh, don't ask me!" she cried. "I can't tell you—I can't!"

"The law requires you to tell me," said Mr. Warble.

"Shame — shame!" cried some one in the crowd.

"Put that man out!" shouted the Judge, angrily. "Let the examination proceed."

Confused with the shock, frightened by the publicity of the situation, and overcome with her emotions, Janet perforce answered the questions of Mr. Warble, denying in toto that Tom had robbed her, but admitting that he was the friend she had referred to, whose voice was like the voice of the train robber; that she had known him for several years,

that he was her father's partner in business,
that she had known him especially well for
the last year or two—yes, that she had been
engaged to him, but no longer was ; that this
engagement had been broken seven weeks
previously, the day before his disappearance ;
that she had not seen or heard anything of
him since ; that she had been greatly worried
—yes, that she couldn't but feel responsible
for anything that might happen to him, since
he had gone off so suddenly after what she
had said to him, and she was afraid, from the
nature of their talk, that he would get into
dangers, perhaps very great dangers, and
that she had hoped in coming West herself
that she might possibly see him and avert
these dangers—and oh, dear! it was too
awful—she couldn't bear it !

She nearly broke down at this point, and
Mr. Warble gave her the opportunity to recover herself before going on.

" You are sure, you say, that the prisoner
was not the train robber, in spite of the
great resemblance of the voices ? "

" Yes."

" You are positive it was some other
man ? "

" Yes."

"Young lady," said Mr. Warble, severely, "you perhaps forget that you are speaking under oath. This is no matter to be regarded lightly. Are you ready to swear that the prisoner could not have been the man who held up your train?"

"I object to this needless questioning," said Colonel Trout. "The witness is aware that she is speaking under oath, and has made her statements accordingly. And I also object, your Honor, to my honorable friend's cross-examination of his own witness in this unseemly and irregular manner."

His Honor, however, upheld the attorney-general, stating that in view of the evident reluctance of the witness he should allow him to put his questions in any form he pleased; and again Mr. Warble asked Janet if she were ready to swear to her last statement.

"I—I am sure he wasn't the train robber."

"But will you swear it?"—in a loud tone and a severe manner.

"I know that he couldn't have been."

"But will you swear it?" Mr. Warble spoke still louder and looked more severe.

"It was really impossible, you see."

"But will you swear it?" Mr. Warble roared the question this time, and his aspect was truly terrible.

"I—I should rather not swear it," said Janet, falteringly. "I know he wasn't the train robber, but—I don't like to swear things."

"Oh, very well, very well," said Mr. Warble, having made his point. "The actual robber was masked, you say, and you could not see his face at all?"

"No."

"Was his figure and general appearance unlike the prisoner's?"

"Perhaps—yes."

"If the prisoner were masked are you sure you would know him?"

"Why—I don't know."

"Was the robber dressed as the prisoner is now?"

"I don't remember exactly."

"Has the prisoner ever worn just such clothes when you have seen him before?"

"No."

"Could you swear that the clothes he has on now were not the ones worn by the train robber?"

" No-o."

" Can you, in fact, mention any one thing that makes it possible for you to show that the prisoner at the bar was not the man who held you up?"

This was the last straw.   Janet could bear no more.   She looked wildly at Tom, at the Judge, the jury, about the crowded court-room, once more at Mr. Warble and then burst into tears.   Jerroray put her arms about her quickly and soothingly patted her back and murmured words of sympathy and comfort.

" We have not heard the witness's answer to the last question," said Mr. Warble, complacently, " but I think we all understand. I have finished with her, and unless Colonel Trout desires to cross-examine her she might be excused."

Tom Norrie whispered energetically to Colonel Trout, who released the witness with apparent reluctance, and upon the proviso that he might call her later for the defence after she had recovered from the severity of the attorney-general's brutal cross-examination.

Then the State called to the witness stand one George M. Drain.   The name was en-

tirely unfamiliar to Tom, but the person who
appeared in answer to it was his old friend
Trilby, of the Den of Thieves. He looked
at Tom with a hateful smile, and calmly
swore that he was the train robber, Tom
Nelson. His story was brief, but telling.
He had known Nelson but six weeks or
thereabouts, had met him several times at
a gambling den in Bloomer, known as the
Yeller Hell, had been invited by him to
join his gang, and had been in all the hold-
ups. But remorse for the wicked life he was
leading, into which he had been drawn by
the fascinations and influence of the prisoner,
being himself but twenty years old, inexper-
ienced and of an artless and confiding nature (here the crowd laughed derisively) had
led him to reflect seriously, and he had finally reached the conviction that the only
way in which he could retrieve his errors
was to give his evil accomplices away to
the State. (Hisses and jeers.) In the last
hold-up, the occasion on which the prisoner
had been captured, he was sent forward
early in the day with two other men to see
that the coast was clear, to board the train
at Aurora, and to stop it at the point agreed
on. The other two men were to conceal

19

themselves on the tender and hold up, at the proper time, the engineer and express agent respectively, while his duty was to follow the conductor out the moment the train slackened, and then hold him up before he could leap from the car.   This was their usual method, though at times they varied it in order to avert suspicion.   He had carried out the program exactly as ordered by his captain, the prisoner, with the one exception that while waiting about Aurora he had called on the sheriff, and then, not finding him, on the city marshal.   The result was than an Arms palace horse-car had been telegraphed for to Bloomer and was attached to the long train just at the moment it drew out from Aurora.   The stop was made about five miles farther on, but the gang of robbers took alarm before the marshal and his posse could get their horses out of the car, and thus, having the start of them, mostly escaped.   The only way he could account for Nelson himself being the one man caught was that some of the others must have reached first the spot where all the horses were fastened, and taken the boss's fleet thoroughbred.   She was fast as the wind, and if he'd been on her they'd never have had a sight of him.

All this story was told with such an indescribable air of cynical hypocrisy and such
evident venom, that its narrator became the
object of the general disgust of the audience.
He was hissed frequently, and such words as
sneak, tell-tale, and traitor were cast at him
in stage whispers by his many ill-wishers in
the crowd.

But he kept his eye on the jury and his
evil, self-satisfied smile never once left him.

" It's Tom Nelson or nothing now," said
Tom Norrie as the court adjourned here for
dinner. Jerroray brought Janet to speak to
him before he was taken back to the jail, and
he had a few moments' talk with her. She
was too agitated to say much, and they were
constrained both by the people about them
and the thought of what had happened at
their last interview. She told him brokenly
of her indignation at being held up. Then
a slight illness of her aunt had kept them in
Salt Lake City, and when they heard there
of the capture of the outlaw all Janet's fighting instincts had come to the fore, and she
had resolved to carry out her threat and
meet him in the court-room as a witness for
the prosecution. She had taken the journey
back alone, much against her aunt's will.

"Glad as I am to have found you, Tom, what I have done simply breaks my heart." Her eyes filled with tears, she could say no more, and Tom was led away from her by his impatient guard.

CHAPTER XIV

As Tom Norrie was brought back into the court-room at two o'clock, the first person he saw was the outlaw himself. He was apparently in the character of the well-dressed and urbane drummer, and he wore the familiar little quizzical smile which had been so important a part of his make-up therein. He nodded pleasantly to Tom, but there was somehow in his look a coolness, or aloofness, Tom could scarcely say what, that sent an instant chill to his heart. In his strong liking for Tom Nelson, under the spell as it were of his charm, and influenced by the unbounded confidence of Jerroray, it had never once entered his head that the outlaw could betray him. He might be unequal to the task of saving him, or even fail to appear at all, but betray him, never ! Now, as the thought flashed across him, Tom saw how completely he was in the man's power, and how unlikely it was that he would sacrifice himself to save a person whom he had not known a fortnight. He thought of hard labor in state-prison for twenty years, and turned sick all through, and closed his eyes and dropped his head on his hand with a sense of terrible faintness. Why had he been so foolhardy, so reckless as to stake his whole life upon a cast—to throw up everything for a momentary pleasure in danger, a foolish idea of proving that he was not a coward?

He might have gone to Cuba and fought with the patriots there for their independence, and died, perhaps, on some battlefield, a hero's death. That would have been a happy ending—but this! And would it break Janet's heart? Would she feel herself to blame?—doubly to blame? Would it spoil her life, too? Ah, he must prevent that at least; he must do something to check her remorse and convince her that she was in no sort responsible. Thinking thus he plucked up courage and faced the situation again, squarely. There was still a chance that Tom Nelson was there as Jack Potts in mere bravado, and that he would amuse himself with riddling the case of the

prosecution with holes and using Mr. Warble as a target for his wit.

Court opened, and Mr. Warble, with an
air of satisfaction that he could not all conceal, called the name of John H. Potts.
Tom Nelson arose, was sworn, and duly
took his place on the witness-stand. The
first part of the examination brought out the
facts that he was a drummer, resident in
Chicago, and travelling for a firm there;
that he had been in Aurora ten days since
and had gone on in the pursuit of his business. Hearing of the capture of the train-
robber he had written his friend Mr. Keach
of his willingness to tell what he knew at
the trial. Mr. Keach, after communicating
with the prosecuting attorney, had informed
him of the time when it would occur; and
at much inconvenience to himself he had
returned from another part of the State to
testify.

Then he narrated rapidly—all the while
in the hoarse voice of Jack Potts, so different from the smooth accents of Tom Nelson
—the occurrences of his first meeting with
the prisoner in the bar-room of the Empire
Hotel at Bud, his immediate recognition of
the likeness of his voice to that of the out-

law, and consequent suspicion that he was not the J. Chance he claimed to be, and his decision to follow him to Aurora on the morning train.   He said that the words and actions of the prisoner grew more and more suspicious, the conversation being largely about the train robber, and about the prisoner's intention to recover from him the diamonds he had taken from Miss Geraldine Roray.   Then when the prisoner dropped his handkerchief, and at once disowned it on having the tell-tale initials of T. N. pointed out to him, he, the witness, no longer had a doubt, and everyone else in the car surmised at once that Mr. Chance was really Tom Nelson.

"I object, your Honor," interrupted Colonel Trout, "to allowing this young man to argue the case himself—especially," he added in his most sardonic manner, "as he deprives my distinguished colleague of the unaccustomed and valued privilege of arguing before a jury."

"Mr. Potts," said the Court, "please confine yourself to what happened.   We don't care to know your suspicions and surmises, or any one else's.   Just tell us the facts as you saw them."

Thus adjured, the outlaw gave briefly the occurrences at the Palace Hotel, and told of his attempt to save the prisoner, and his suggestion to him to get out of the way as quick as he could.   Then he narrated, just as they happened, the escape and his pretended pursuit in order to divert ill will from himself; while Tom Norrie marvelled at his cleverness throughout in not once perjuring himself.

" Have you seen the prisoner since?" asked Mr. Warble.

" I have," declared the witness.

" Tell just where and when."

" My business took me on the train at the time of the last hold-up, the night on which the prisoner was caught, and though masked, I saw him close at hand and recognized him instantly.   He saw me and knows that I recognized him.   He cannot deny that he was there."   Tom Nelson looked directly at Tom Norrie as he said this, and our hero turned pale at the cold perfidy of his smile.

Colonel Trout, with all his fighting instincts aroused, began at once on the cross-examination.   He started in to make the outlaw confess first that he was no drummer, and that his pretence to be so was merely a cover for other and less legitimate business.

But Tom Nelson was ready for him at every turn, produced on demand his notebook and record of sales, and even called up an Aurora jeweller in the audience, who would testify that he had sold him a bill of goods only ten days before. The colonel was appalled at this cleverness and foresight.

"The man's too smart for us," he said aside to Tom. "If we cross-examine him on the hold-up he'll be all ready for us there, as he has been here, and just clinch the whole thing tighter. I'll ask him one more question in order to get in Miss Roray's evidence later, and then I'll drop him like a hot potato and be glad to be done with him." He turned once more to the witness. "Did you not on the day of the escape of the prisoner from Aurora make the statement that he was not Tom Nelson?"

"I can't remember particularly saying anything of that sort," said Jack Potts, easily, but assuming a puzzled expression.

"Oh, very well, that's enough," said the colonel, with all the air of being victor, rather than vanquished.

Jack Potts sat down, and Mr. Warble declared, triumphantly:

"The prosecution rests."

After the usual formal motion on the part
of Colonel Trout to dismiss the indictment
and discharge the prisoner because of the
entire lack of evidence against him, and an
equally formal denial on the part of the
Court, the case for the defence began.

Colonel Trout did not spend much on
flourish in his opening address, but after
calling the jury's attention to the superlative
and gilt-edged respectability of the firm to
which his client belonged, as evidenced by
the enormous volume of their business, noted,
with telling brevity, the points he proposed
to make to controvert those of the prosecution.   He pointed out the ridiculous aspect
of the so-called evidence brought in to prove
that the prisoner was the author of the latest
hold-up.   Then, claiming that he had shown
conclusively that they couldn't even prove
that he was there at all, he stated that his
client, however, was perfectly willing to admit that he was there, would explain how
and why, and was anxious, in short, to tell
his whole story on the witness-stand.   The
prisoner's fearless and confident innocence
had been a lesson to him through his brief
association with him.   He desired to tell the
entire truth to the jury with the most com-

plete frankness, and contrary as this was to
the usual course of procedure, he, Colonel
Trout, was perforce won over to a reluctant
but absolute belief in its advisability in this
particular case.   Telling the truth, then,
would be the case for the defence; and after that they would conclusively prove that
at the time of the four previous hold-ups
the prisoner had been far from Rising Sun
County, and could not possibly be the author
of this tremendous conspiracy.

So Tom told his truthful tale of the last six
eventful weeks of his life, touching briefly
upon his whereabouts on the three earliest
dates, becoming fuller in details after his arrival at Bud on the night of the fourth robbery, retailing Tom Nelson's own story to
him of the inner meaning of the happenings
on the train and in Aurora, and giving a full
and graphic account of all the later occurrences.

The crowd smiled at his statements about
the wonderful black mare that Jack Potts
brought him to escape on, and about that
gentleman's direction of him to so equivocal
a place of safety.   They were sympathetic-
ally amused at the account of his reception
in the robber's camp by the robber's gang,

and they liked the story of Trilby's thrashing.   But they smiled again when he stated
that it was because of the thrashing that
Trilby had a spite against him, and swore
now that he was Tom Nelson.   Then he told
them that at the time of the fifth train robbery he was left behind at the Den, in the
custody of the hostler, the Chinaman, and
the boy, and they laughed outright.   And, in
spite of the Judge's reprimand, they laughed
again when he said he went to the sixth as
a prisoner, and unarmed ; that at the time
of the alarm and the hurried escape he had,
of his own motion, given himself up to be
caught, to save his friend Tom Nelson ; and
that the only thing he had refused, and must
still refuse to tell, because of the hospitality
there received, was the whereabouts of the
Den of Thieves.   The perfidy of his friend
might seem to absolve him from all such
necessity of good faith, yet his own sense of
honor in the matter was too strong to permit
this.

But though the crowd would not take his
tale seriously he was not to be shaken on
cross-examination ; and Jerroray's evidence,
following at once upon his own, and strictly
corroborating it all, so far as it went, made

a very evident good impression.   Colonel
Trout managed to bring in with her story a
great deal to cast suspicion on Jack Potts,
yet in such a way as to give the helpless and
indignant Mr. Warble no chance to object.
Then at the end he said :

" You have heard Mr. Potts's evidence to
the effect that the prisoner is Tom Nelson ? "

" Yes."

" Have you ever had any conversation
with him on that subject ? "

" I should smile !   He told me in so many
words, on the day he helped Chance to get
away from my house, that he warn't Tom
Nelson ; that he knew it, an' could prove it
to me, but he hadn't time then, because he
had to go after him.   An' he said he was
an Eastern tenderfoot, an' a Harvard man,
out here on a lark under an assumed name."
(Great sensation in court-room.)

" Was that all he said ? "

" Well, it was enough to make me as cock-
sure as he was.   But then I had another
reason for bein' certain he was right."

" Oh, you had ?   Well, tell us what this
reason was."

" About the best you could get.   I've seen
the real Tom Nelson."

"You have known Tom Nelson and talked with him?"

"Yes, sir, I have."

"Under his own name?"

"Well, not exactly!"

"Under what name, then?"

"Under the name of Jack Potts."

"That will do," said Colonel Trout, and Jerroray sat down amid increased sensation.

"I have not finished with the witness," said Mr. Warble, severely. "Miss Roray, you say that my witness, this estimable gentleman, Mr. John H. Potts, is Tom Nelson. How do you know this?"

"Because I'm sure of it."

"Well, but how are you sure of it?"

"Because I know it." Everybody laughed and Mr. Warble became more severe.

"Have you ever addressed him as Tom Nelson?"

"Why, no-o!" said Jerroray, surprised by the question.

"Has he himself ever admitted to you that he was Tom Nelson?"

"Well—he didn't need to——"

"Answer directly," said Mr. Warble, repeating the question, and Jerroray was obliged to say that he hadn't.

" Did some one tell you, then, that he was Tom Nelson ? "

" Did you think I just guessed ? " said Jerroray, derisively, but was again pinned down to the categorical response.

" Was it possibly the prisoner, Mr. Chance, who told you so."

" Well, yes ; he has told me."

" Has anybody else told you so ? "

" I don't know 's anybody else has."

" That's all, that's all," said Mr. Warble, briskly.

Biddy and Ernest were called to confirm Jerroray's evidence, which they did effectually. Biddy told an excellent story of Micky's connection with the gentleman who had testified as John H. Potts, and how he'd made Micky, and she liked him herself, and didn't want to go back on him, but divil a bit would she let him send an innocent man to prison and cut up high jinks with her Jerry's affections. She didn't know whether he was any train robber or not—she'd never seen him rob trains—and she wasn't sure whether his name was Potts or Nelson or Jones or Smith, but he owned the black mare, that was straight. Micky'd run away so he needn't testify to it, and she presumed

Micky might know his name, but she didn't know all Micky knew, any more'n he knew all she knew, and she hoped anyway nobody'd ever go to state-prison on account of what either of 'em knew, and she'd oughter go home an' finish up her bakin' instead of sittin' 'round here with a court and wastin' all her time.

" She's your witness, Warble," said the colonel, when the laugh had subsided.

" I don't want her," said Mr. Warble, in a tone so genuine that everybody laughed again.

The colonel, in trying to establish the prisoner's good character, succeeded in bringing out through Janet the fact that in the pious city of his birth Mr. Norrie was considered an estimable young man, and that no one would have thought of his turning train robber. But his brilliant idea, born of the evidence she had given for the prosecution, was simply to prove that the prisoner was too great a coward anyway to dream of doing anything of the sort. In this attempt he succeeded in making Janet very angry and Jerroray still angrier, and eliciting from both violent statements of the extreme intrepidity of the prisoner.

20

The evidence that attempted to prove that
Tom was not there on the occasion of the
four first robberies came next, and, as Tom
had feared, was very shaky evidence.   He
had not reflected when he kept such doubtful company that he was destined to be
known by it, so greatly to his own detri-
ment, and so soon.

When the defence rested Mr. Warble immediately called Jack Potts in rebuttal.

"When Colonel Trout asked you if you
had ever stated that the prisoner was not
Tom Nelson you were unable to recollect.
Has Miss Roray's evidence that you made
that statement to her refreshed your memory?"

"It has.   I now remember telling her
so."

"Please give your reasons for a statement
so contradictory to all your evidence in the
trial to-day?"

Then the outlaw, with a clever assumption
of confusion and embarrassment, explained
that he was very much taken with Miss
Roray; that he saw how her imagination
was fired by the thought of Tom Nelson and
his exploits, and how the idea that Mr.
Chance might be the train robber had visibly

inclined her toward him ; and that thus, on
the basis of any ruse being fair in love, he
had simply told her what he did in order
that he might have a fair chance to make
her like him as much as she already liked
his rival—darting one bold look at her—
which would be impossible so long as she
thought Mr. Chance was the train robber.

This plausible explanation had a most convincing sound.   Even Jerroray was puzzled
by it, and looked from one young man to
the other, as if she hardly knew the truth.
Janet, sitting by her side, grew very anxious, and whispered to her eagerly, but Jerroray only shook her head vaguely, as if her
own uncertainties prevented her from resolv-
ing another's.

It was no use, thought Tom Norrie.   The
game was up, the day was lost.   It had
rested with Tom Nelson, and Tom Nelson
had betrayed him.   He was to go to state-
prison in the outlaw's place.   He remembered how deeply but a brief time since he
had pitied a man he knew for his sentence
of two years at hard labor—it seemed so bitter a thing, somehow, for an educated man
of delicate tastes and luxurious habits—and
now ten years of it, at least, lay before him,

and perhaps twenty—practically his whole
life.   He could not listen to what followed
—it passed as in a dream.   He heard laugh-
ter now, and then cheers or hisses—but they
made no impression on him.   This was his
last day in the big, bright world ; he was going to be buried alive, and he should never
see Janet again.   He forgot Jerroray, he
forgot Tom Nelson's perfidy, he forgot everything except Janet—never had he realized
until then how much he loved her.

Colonel Trout filled all the interstices of
his summing-up with covert ridicule, not
alone of the eminent counsel for the prosecution, but of Boreal, the small provincial town
in which he resided, and which had actually
had the impudence to imagine itself Bloomer's rival when the capital of the State was
selected.   The colonel had a fine gift for
sarcasm, and he screwed Mr. Warble up to
such a pitch of writhing, heated indignation
that he in turn provided the audience with a
great laugh when he rose to reply to Colonel
Trout and nearly lost control of himself in
the process.   Words failed him, and for some
moments an inarticulate sputtering of intense earnestness was all that he could produce.

But the tragedy of the case was not lost sight of in the humorous aspects of the counsel engaged. Colonel Trout was pre-eminent as an advocate, and he put the case to the jury with an impassioned spirit that seemed almost to shake them.   He pointed out the sheer nonsense of the idea that a man would be able in so short a time to come out of the East, get together a gang, and conduct train robberies so successfully, on so large a scale, without an ounce of experience beyond a tame business life in what was reputed to be even the tamest of tame Eastern cities.   To sacrifice such a young man, heedless and reckless, perhaps, but innocent through and through, to a cool desperado like the man who had given evidence as Jack Potts—this would be a cruel trick to play under the name of justice.

He showed clearly the absurdity of thinking that so clever a man as Tom Nelson would travel about in the way in which it had been proved that the prisoner did, with a large valise full of his belongings, all clearly marked with his initials.   Tom Nelson, going over the road directly after one of his robberies to hear what people might say of him, would carry with him the least possible luggage, after the manner of the so-called Jack Potts, being then always ready for instant flight, and leaving no incriminating evidence behind him.

Moreover, the real robber would be no such fool as to pretend that he had never heard of the train robberies, and then talk of nothing but of them and their perpetrator ; whereas a young man like Mr. Norrie, coming in search of adventures from the tame East to the wild West, would have behaved exactly so ; nothing could be more natural than his interest in the whole matter.

A guilty man, too, would have been frightened by the demonstrations in the bar-room of the Palace Hotel, and would have got out of town inside of ten minutes after getting out of the hotel. The prisoner, on the contrary, calmly went to drink afternoon tea— afternoon tea, gentlemen — with a young lady, who happened also to be the sheriff's daughter. Did that look like a guilty conscience or a clear one?

Again, when the prisoner was captured after the last hold-up, was not his own round unvarnished tale corroborated by the facts of his being unarmed and mounted on an inferior nag, when it was known that the train robber himself rode the best horse in all the country side?

"Gentlemen of the jury, in the prisoner at the bar, my unfortunate, innocent, and maligned client, the State recognizes its last chance. For over a month it has been, as it were, held at bay, by the most audacious and accomplished villain that ever defied its authority. The State cannot catch Tom Nelson, but its pride is at stake and it must catch somebody. So it apprehends an unarmed and peaceful citizen, and bends all its energies to sending him to state-prison. It amounts to a conspiracy, gentlemen, a conspiracy to sacrifice an innocent man to save the pride of the government. If you or I, gentlemen, had been riding our favorite horse on that prairie, on that evening, we, too, should have been caught and declared to be Tom Nelson.

"Now let me tell you how it all occurred. Your most admirable sheriff, a gentleman celebrated in his official capacity throughout the whole State, is unfortunately out of town when word is brought of the hold-up to occur on a certain train at a certain time. But the city marshal of Aurora, instead of sending off post haste after him, as might

easily have been done, is delighted with a
chance of distinguishing himself—which, we
may remark parenthetically, he has most effectually accomplished.   He gets together a
large band of brave men, arms them to the
teeth, and they set forth to hold up the
hold-uppers, if I may coin the word.   But
do they do it as men of sense would do it ?
—seat themselves like passengers in the forward car and seize the robbers the moment
they appear ?   Not a bit—not a bit, gentlemen !   They take along a lot of useless
horses and tie themselves on to the end of
the train.   They think they may as well
combine pleasure with business and have an
evening canter ; and anyhow they are safer
on horseback, at a distance from the robbers,
than within close range of their guns.   So
they bungle the thing about as bad as it
could be bungled, and let the whole gang of
robbers get away in the darkness.   Half a
dozen schoolboys, gentlemen, could have
caught those train robbers, but the city
marshal of Aurora, with the entire police
force of the city, with deputies and horses
and all his supposed experience and his wonderful courage, he was powerless to get one
of 'em.   So then Marshal Gosling says to

his men : ' Now we've come out with all
these horses and all this flourish we can't go
back without somebody ; the people back in
Aurora wouldn't like it.   We've got to find
a man.   Any kind of a man will do, but a
man we must have.'   So then they cruise
around a while and finally light on the
prisoner.   And the marshal says to his deputies : ' Now he looks like Tom Nelson,
he acts like Tom Nelson, and he speaks like
Tom Nelson.   Let's call him Tom Nelson ! '
So then they have a christening and return
to Aurora with flying colors.   And my innocent client, sacrificed first to save the
pride of the city marshal of Aurora, is now
being sacrificed again to save the pride of
the attorney-general of the State.   If this,
gentlemen, is justice, let us demand injustice ;
if this is right, let us on our bended knees
sue for wrong ! ''

" And to take as conclusive evidence
against the prisoner the testimony of such a
confessed criminal as the man named Drain,"
went on the colonel—" a creature known by
so low and common a nickname as Trilby,
which in itself was enough to place him
morally among the vilest scoundrels—yet a
man, too, who looked the name, if any one

could—who might, in short, be said to be a Trilby of the deepest dye—a man whose malice and libel were amply accounted for by the severe thrashing given him by the prisoner—to take the evidence of such an abandoned animal, a branded sneak and informer, and put it before that of two such exemplary, innocent, and high-minded young people as Miss Geraldine Roray and the prisoner—this was indeed a crime against justice.

" Look on the guileless and noble face of the prisoner, gentlemen of the jury, and then on the scheming wickedness of the countenance of John H. Potts — look on them both, consider well, and then, if you can, send the innocent to jail and let the criminal go free ! Tear this young man from the arms of a lady who loves him, break up two sweet young lives, cast an awful gloom on a great commercial name of untarnished business integrity, interfere with nature, youth, love, domestic joy, trade, and credit, and then, if you can, call yourselves ever again honest American citizens ! "

The colonel sat down mopping his brow, flushed and self - satisfied, after this impassioned appeal.   The crowd cheered him and some tender-hearted ladies and gentlemen wept over his eloquence.

Hope sprang once more in the hearts of Jerroray and Janet. The decision of the jury was again in doubt.

The eloquent speech of Mr. Warble, the Judge's charge—neither of them could dim this hope. Then the jury went out, the twelve arbiters of a man's whole life, and every one in the audience asked his neighbor what the verdict would be. There seemed at least half a chance for the prisoner, so gallant and good-looking a young man, sitting there with his eyes fixed mournfully on the face of the young Eastern lady, who surely loved him now, whatever she had done seven weeks before. The color had come back into her dark face since Colonel Trout's strong effort for the prisoner, and sitting as she did, side by side with Jerroray, such a contrast to her brilliant fairness and bloom, she made part of an uncommon picture. Jack Potts sat within two feet of them, close at Jerroray's hand, but though she had smiled at him with a dazzling sweetness on her first sight of him, she had looked at him but once since he had given his testimony, and then only to throw into his eyes a glance of flashing scorn.   He had smiled even then, and was smiling still, that little quiet smile that gave him a look of such coolness and mastery and cynical indifference.   Jerroray stole a secret sidewise look at him now.

"I suppose it's natural you should think. I was in love with your Tom, bein' as you're in love with him yourself," she said to Janet. "And of course, I do like him awful well, an' we've been awful good chums this jail trip.   But, my!—I never saw but one man who could stir me all up inside and out—an' that's the one, that Jack Potts, who's Tom Nelson just as sure as I'm Jerry Roray.   I could have loved him.   Somehow he just strikes me all of a heap, first one way and then t'other, for I hate him now just as much as I did like him.   An' yet all the time I can't believe that he won't get Tom Norrie off.   I feel sure he can do anything he wants to, an' that he wants to do that.   But if he don't I'll never speak a decent word to him so long as I live—I swear it!   I could stand a coward better'n a sneak that gives away his chums that trust him."

A sudden movement cut short Jerroray's further remarks—for though but ten minutes had passed the jury were coming back.

Breathless stillness held everyone, as they moved into the room. Even Tom waked from his lethargy and turned to look at them with almost a ray of hope in his heart. They were looking at him, too, and the foreman caught his eye as the clerk put to him the usual formal questions, and faltered in the words he was about to speak, and looked about him in sudden embarrassment. Then in a moment more he recovered himself and delivered the verdict.

"Guilty!"

Yes, of course—it was all over—what else could have been expected?—Tom asked himself. He looked about the court-room in a dazed way, and again his eyes fell upon the familiar, yet unfamiliar, face he had seen before in the crowd. The man was looking directly at him, with a sort of friendly grin, and in this moment of emotion it flashed across Tom that it was Snide—Snide with his beard shaved off, and in store clothes, yet unmistakably Snide none the less. He looked toward Nelson in a meaning way, and Tom followed his eyes. He looked back and Snide nodded, then fixed his eyes on someone far front in the crowd, and again Tom followed only to see Button.

The same process was gone through once more, and this time it was Gully's red head, now close-cropped, by which our hero's eyes were refreshed.   Snide had apparently other human facts to communicate, but some one nudged the prisoner, and he found that the clerk was addressing him, and asking him if he had anything to say before receiving sentence.

"Only what I have said before," said Tom, rising and speaking with quiet firmness, "that I am an innocent man.   My own recklessness, and the perfidy of a man I liked and trusted have put me in this compromising situation.   I can see, myself, how much it all looks against me, but I ought to be given the benefit of the doubt.   Tom Nelson, alias Jack Potts, is the man who should go to prison—not I."

Colonel Trout pleaded warmly with the court for as light a sentence as possible, mentioning the youth and previous unblemished record of his client, Mr. Norrie, his excellent connections, his position, and his prospects.

The Judge, plainly moved, said however, that in many eyes all these condoning circumstances might be thought aggravating ones—the great opportunities of the prisoner making his responsibilities toward society only the greater.

"You have had a fair trial and been found guilty," he said, looking at Tom, and speaking with hesitation, almost as if he were apologizing for justice. The prisoner's frank and serious face was so convincingly innocent that it was with an evident effort that his Honor continued : "It is the sentence of this court that you be confined in the state-prison at Bloomer, at hard labor, for the term of twenty years."

Janet gave a wild cry that rang through the court-room. She covered her face with her hands and bent her head in complete abandon upon Jerroray's lap. Jerroray sat bolt upright, white as a white rose, and red as a red one by turns, her arms thrown close about the form of poor Janet, shaken in its grief. She turned her head and darted one burning look of scorn at Nelson, and met in his eye a smile of so subtle meaning that it made her heart stand still with a sudden revulsion of feeling.

"There's still life, and therefore hope," he murmured. He rose, looked deliberately about the crowded court-room, then finally at the Judge, and asked for permission to speak a few words which might establish the innocence of the prisoner. Strange as the request was, and without precedent, there was something so significant in the man's face and voice that the Court could not deny him.

" It is an unusual thing to ask, and an unusual thing to permit," said his Honor, " but the peculiarities of the case, the relation in which you stand to it, and a strong sense of the innocence and integrity of the prisoner in spite of the damning evidence against him, lead me to grant it. Yet you are aware that in knowing the prisoner to be innocent, yet swearing to his guilt, you have perjured yourself, and are hence guilty of grave contempt of court."

Tom Nelson bowed. " So it might seem," he said, the assumed hoarseness gone from his tones at last ; and as he spoke Janet lifted her head with a startled look.

" The voice ! The real voice ! " she cried. She looked at Tom, who was suddenly smiling, at Jerroray, who was radiant, at the crowd struck with her cry and agog with sudden expectancy of something abnormal about to happen.

" So it might seem," repeated Tom Nelson, bland, suave, and master of the situation. " But your Honor nevertheless mistakes. My contempt, if I have it, is in no sort contempt of you or of your august court, but rather the contempt of an outlaw for all law, for the travesty of justice which rants up and down the little legal stage. But if your Honor will condescend to look over the record of my evidence you will see that I have nowhere perjured myself. I related things exactly as they happened, and in no place did I state that the prisoner was Tom Nelson. That inference was in the minds of those who heard what I said, and makes of all this a very suggestive commentary on the value of circumstantial evidence. For while I have said only what is true, and am guilty neither of perjury nor of contempt of court, yet the prisoner was practically convicted by my testimony, and I am myself, all the while, Tom Nelson, the train robber. [Great sensation.] Mr. Norrie, the prisoner at the bar, saved my life at great risk to his own last week, and I am come today, as I promised him then, to save him from the consequences. He has been reckless and brave, but is entirely innocent of

21

any and all the crimes for which he has been
so unjustly convicted.'' Tom Nelson pronounced these last words slowly and with
strong emphasis, like an actor who wishes to
make sure that his point is not missed, and
in truth the crowd broke at once into tu-
multuous cheering, and it was some minutes before the Judge could bring them to
order.

" This is a most remarkable confession,
at a most remarkable time,'' he said. ''In
all my twenty years on the bench I have
known of nothing like it.'' He spoke
gravely, almost with emotion ; then turned
to Colonel Trout and asked him if he had
any suggestions to make.

The colonel rose with great alacrity, stating that he agreed with his Honor that it
was a most extraordinary occurrence, and,
it seemed to him, required extraordinary action on the part of the court. ''I will
therefore move you, sir, that the conviction
and sentence of my client be vacated ; and,
that the procedure may be orderly, I will
first make a motion for a new trial, on the
ground of this newly discovered evidence
and the manifest mistake that has been made.
And if the attorney-general insists in putting

the county to further expense in the endeavor to convict an innocent man, I shall ask you to let the prisoner go on his own recogniz- ance pending this trial. And I ask that, contrary to the usual rule of procedure, this motion be heard and disposed of at once.''

The Judge said that he was ready to com- ply with these very reasonable suggestions, unless the attorney-general had some valid objections.

The county prosecutor was talking to Mr. Warble with great warmth, evidently trying hard to convince him of something, and as that gentleman said nothing in response to the Judge's remark, Colonel Trout asked that Tom Nelson be sworn upon this motion. The outlaw made his full confession under oath, telling his story briefly, humorously, and in that '' takin' '' way that Jerroray had already noted as one of his pleasing features. He compelled sympathy by his very man- ner, and the crowd, listening breathlessly to every word, was altogether with him long before he finished. They applauded all the jokes he made, and every expression of re- volt against the existing order of society. These expressions were chiefly directed against his own parent, to whom he sent several vivacious messages through the news-paper reporters present.

Snide and Gully were called by Colonel Trout, at Nelson's suggestion, to corroborate his testimony. Then the colonel, after consulting a moment with the outlaw, stated that there were ten or more other witnesses to testify to the same facts, but that he should prefer not to trouble the court further—unless, he added, sarcastically, the other side should make it necessary by their case—whatever it might be.

Mr. Warble replied pompously, in response to the Judge's question, that he should call no witnesses in opposition to the motion.

The Judge thereupon announced that he should grant the motion for a new trial, adding that the conviction and sentence were thereby set aside. He then spoke slowly and judicially for some moments, suggesting that if the attorney-general were willing, there hardly need be another trial. After this extraordinary confession under oath, it would be very unlikely to find a jury who would convict, and the seemingly needless expense to the county would be great. If the attorney-general wished time to consider—

Mr. Warble arose with greater airs of importance than ever, though mingled now with an evident sense of bitter injury, and said that his only desire was to see justice done, as he had stated in his opening. He should prefer to leave the matter in the hands of the Court, and would cheerfully acquiesce in any decision it might arrive at. He had come into the case after it was entirely prepared by his able young friend, the county prosecutor, and had himself nothing to do with getting up the evidence. If he had seen Mr. Potts before he went on the stand all might have been otherwise and a serious blunder obviated. And he had just succeeded in convincing his young friend that the interests of justice would be better subserved by the entry of a nol. pros. in the case of the State against this false Tom Nelson — keeping his eye, as he said so, upon the real Nelson, who smiled at him pleasantly.

"Mr. Clerk," said his Honor at once, "you may make the entry of nol. pros. and the order of the court that the prisoner be honorably discharged." He turned to Tom Norrie and apologized to him in a dignified way on behalf both of the court and of the people of the county, congratulating him on his release and winding up with a few eloquent remarks which were at once applauded by the excited and happy crowd. The Judge smiled indulgently on these demonstrations, and did not check them, being well aware of his own eloquence and of the necessary results upon an audience of giving it rein.

Mr. Warble, on the contrary, being anxious to speak, was greatly annoyed. As soon as the noise subsided he made himself heard, with crushing dignity. " Your Honor will, of course, order this hardened scoundrel, the real Tom Nelson, into the custody of the sheriff, charged with the crimes that he has confessed committing ? "

" I so order," said the Judge, " and the sheriff will do his duty."

The Terror of Aurora, who had seemed very uneasy for some time and had kept his eye fixed upon the outlaw, started with great eagerness to do as he was bid. He had hardly reached his feet before Tom Nelson, with a smile, threw one arm high in the air, and upon the signal fifteen or twenty masked men immediately rose from the crowd at various points throughout the room, and fifteen or twenty revolvers, following the direction of the outlaw's eyes, were fixed upon the sheriff as a target. In the general excitement no one had noticed the masks going on, and every one was taken by surprise; many of the women screamed and some of the men turned pale. The sheriff, however, only took on a more determined look, and, ripping out several striking oaths and two revolvers as well, vowed he'd do his duty if he died on the field, and called on all good citizens to help him. Riot and bloodshed might have been the order of the day in less than five seconds had not Jerroray, radiant with excitement and happiness, opportunely interfered.

"Oh, now, Terence Roray, just you come off!" she said, approaching him with an air of cool command. "What can one dog do against twenty? The court ain't armed, sure, 'cause it's against the law to carry concealed weapons, an' if the court ain't law-abidin', who is? So you've got nobody to back you up, an' you better just put away your gun. Tom Nelson's an awful popular gent, an' we're all on his side here. So if you don't want to turn your dear little toes up in the cold all alone, you'd better hand your barkers over to me. I don't want to

lose my daddy, an' I'll take good care you
don't get 'em back again pretty quick.
Come, there's a good dad," she said, wheed-
lingly, grabbing at the revolvers, " give 'em
up to your little girl like an obedient parent
—I always know what's best for you, Terence."

She had already unbuckled his belt and
holsters, and now as he yielded to her with
a shamefaced laugh, she herself put them on
with ostentatious airs of unconsciousness before the crowd, and wrapped the belt a second time about her hour-glass waist in order
to be able to buckle it at all.   The crowd
was delighted and set up three cheers for
Jerroray, while she stood laughing, in full
view, as pleased as a child.

" Now, gentlemen, give her three cheers
again," said Tom Nelson, " as the ' outlaw's
bride ' this time."

" Gracious ! "   cried Jerroray,   " what
cheek you drummers have got ! You haven't
even asked me yet."

" But you told me to my face that you
were in love with Tom Nelson."

" That was rather a giveaway," she admitted.

" And besides—here are your diamonds."

" Well, that settles it," she said. " I'm
yours. But if you'd really been the sneak
to go back on Tom Norrie you'd never have
laid a finger on me ! "

She took his arm and the crowd gave her
three cheers, and then three more for Mr.
and Mrs. Nelson.

" That sounds nice," said the outlaw.
" We may as well get it fixed up right off.
Mr. Roray, will you give the bride away ? "

The sheriff looked about at the array of
revolvers. " Well, yes. I suppose I may as
well," he replied, and the crowd laughed.

" Will you marry us, Judge ? "

The Judge, looking on with placid but irresponsible interest, was startled.

" Who, I ? I never did such a thing in
my life," he said. " Don't know how, and
couldn't think of it."

" We'll take it as a particular favor if you
do all the same," said Tom Nelson, genially.
" The mayor's on hand, and he'll tell you
how."

The Judge, like the sheriff, took a discreet
glance at the revolvers and consented. With
the mayor to prompt him he managed to
perform the ceremony very creditably, and
then received his reward in the shape of a

most unexpected and resounding kiss from the new Mrs. Nelson. The crowd shouted and cat-called again in wild joy.

"I'd kiss the jury, too, if I wasn't afraid they'd be embarrassed," said the bride, "but you've got to have one anyhow, Terence," and she enfolded the sheriff in a violent embrace. "I hate to leave my good old dad, but I expect it'll be better for me and my husband's health to take a right smart of a weddin' trip."

"I shall miss you awful, Jerry," said the sheriff, with feeling.

"Not a bit more'n I'll miss you, Terence —but you'll come to see us bime-by when things ain't quite so lively. Say," she said suddenly to Tom Norrie, "don't you want to get married too?"

"Nobody would think of marrying me," he replied, with a laugh.

Then Janet did something that she is proud of now whenever she thinks of it, though she can never understand how she came to be brave enough to do it before all those people. "I will marry you, Tom—if you want me," she said, with grave dignity, and flushed at the cheers which rung out in her honor.

"It's the wish of my life," he declared.

He advanced and took her hand and kissed it reverently. "You won't regret it?" he whispered.

"Never!" she declared. "You're the bravest man I ever knew."

The mayor performed the second ceremony, it being rather rough on the poor Judge to work him so hard, as Tom Nelson explained, and the second couple not having the same sentimental reasons for wishing him to do the job for them.

"Now," said Tom Nelson to the crowd, "we want to get out of this. The question is, have we got to do it by force or are you all goin' to help?"

"We'll stand by you!"

"You're a peach!"

"We'll see you through!"

"Hurrah for Tom Nelson!"

These and many other expressions of sympathy poured out on the evening air, and Mr. Nelson looked pleased.

"That's good," he said. "Now, gentlemen, my idea is this. The express goes through here in half an hour, and I would suggest that we escort Mr. and Mrs. Norrie to the train in a body (cheers), and see them off on their weddin' tour (redoubled cheers). But to effect this pleasin' little plan it will be necessary to keep Aurora's Terror, my esteemed father-in-law, agreeably entertained in the interim, for I see he still has business in his eye." He called thereupon for volunteers, formed them into a committee to entertain the sheriff, and suggested the Palace Hotel bar-room as a suitable spot for the festivities. Handing over a lot of money to Mr. Cutler Keach, he asked him to provide the sheriff and party, and all the rest of the crowd, with their favorite drinks, and as much of them as they could get down.

"There'll still be somethin' left over," he said, "but you can keep that to expend on your further education as a detective. I think you can do a little in that line some time, if you work hard," he added, with a smile.

Trilby was then handed over to the crowd with recommendations to their mercy.

"He ain't worth killin'," said Tom Nelson. "Just duck him, or give him a little coat of tar and feathers, or somethin' of that sort. He's a d——d sneak, but things have turned out so well that I don't bear him any grudge."

Mr. Nelson shook hands pleasantly with the attorney-general, Colonel Trout, and the Judge—a ceremony performed with humor by the Court, cordiality by the colonel, and a stiff resistance on the part of Mr. Warble. Tom Norrie followed his example in two of the cases, and settled also the natural anxieties of his counsel in regard to proper payment for his services.

Then, bidding an affectionate good-by to to all the court, they set out for the station, amid the wildest enthusiasm on the part of the crowd. And as the train drew out, bearing one bride and groom to Salt Lake City, they saw the other two set off on horseback for the land called Safety, attended by Gully and Snide, while Micky, who had brought Folly and the Red Devil, wiped away several tears on his sleeve. Everybody cheered, and thus came to an end the greatest sensation Rising Sun County had ever known.

CHAPTER XV

Two weeks later, in the golden afternoon
of a perfect day, Tom and Janet were resting from a long climb by the banks of a little mountain lake. The trees on the shore
were spreading and picturesque, with open
spaces between them, and a short wood-
land grass grew everywhere, golden green as
the sun lay upon it, emerald and blue in the
deep shadows of the trees. Tom, in knick-
erbockers, was stretched at full length on his
back under a huge white oak, with a protrud-
ing root of the tree for a pillow. Janet, in
short skirt and leggings, sat close by in the
attitude of the dying gladiator, resting on
one hand, while with the other she absently pulled up the grass, leaf by leaf.

They had just received that morning, as
they were setting out from the hotel for their
day's jaunt, a naïve and characteristic epistle from Jerroray, telling of the excitements

of their honeymoon on the wing, and of their adventurous plans for the future—Cuba first, for "some real up and down fighting," and then a season of "melting the coin" in "Paree," where they hoped "Terence" would join them, and possibly Tom and Janet also. Our hero and heroine had discussed these pleasant plans a little at the time, but now had not mentioned either the outlaw or his bride for several hours. And for the last ten minutes they had not spoken at all.

"Tom," said Janet, finally, "I can't see what kept you from falling in love with Jerroray."

"Neither can I," responded Tom at once, his eyes fixed on a brown thrush hopping about among the leafy branches over his head.

Janet looked a little dashed at the promptness of this agreement with her views. "She was so extraordinarily good-looking," she went on, however, in a moment, "and so good-tempered and kind and sympathetic, and so quick-witted and sharp, and so really intelligent by nature, and not vulgar in spite of the vulgar people she had lived with all her life, and so clear-headed and sensible, and so jolly and so amusing and droll——"

" I should think you had learned Soule's synonymes by heart," remarked Tom.

" Well, I can't see it at all."

" Neither can I—when I'm not looking at it." Tom rose to a sitting posture, and looked directly at his wife. " Now, however, it's very visible," he observed.

" Oh ! " said Janet, with a world of pleasant enlightenment in her voice.

Tom clasped his knees, still looking at Janet. " I may as well confess that I tried hard to fall in love with her, but though I was sure that you were nothing to me, I couldn't get you out of my head."

Janet looked as if this were a gratifying fact. " It would have served me right if you had," she said.

" But you really wouldn't have cared much," said Tom, after a moment's silence. " It was only the dramatic way the thing happened that made you think you liked me again. I never ought to have taken so base an advantage of you as to marry you at such a moment of excitement."

" Tom," said Janet, gravely, laying her hand upon his arm, " the excitement had nothing to do with it. I knew the moment you left me, that last evening at home, that

I had made an awful mistake; that I loved
you more than I ever did; that it was because I loved you that I had felt and behaved as I did. I could think of nothing
but you day and night, and I had made up
my mind, Tom, that if you took me at my
word and let me go, and never came back,
that I—well, that I should appear in the
rôle of Strephon again, and go after you!''

Tom now looked as gratified as Janet had
done a moment since, but his expression of
this feeling was of a purely inarticulate
nature.

After a few moments Janet reopened the
conversation. "There's one thing you said
that I want to go back to. Why did you
try to fall in love with Jerroray?"

"Oh," said Tom, "that's very compli-
cated. There were lots of reasons."

"Well, tell me them all."

"Oh, they wouldn't all interest you, but
I'll tell you some of them."

"I insist on having them all."

"One reason," said Tom, ignoring this
last speech, "was to prove to myself that I
was utterly indifferent to you. I was confident, of course, that I was so, but still the
positive proof would be pleasant."

22

"Well?" said Janet, smiling.

"Another was that she was so good-looking."

Janet stopped smiling. "Do you really think looks are of any importance when you love a person?" she inquired, with an air of fine scorn.

"Oh, no, not important, but it's pleasant to have a good-looking person around all the time, you know."

Janet grew thoughtful. "Tom," she said, and then stopped.

"Well?" asked Tom.

"Oh, nothing—I was just going to ask you a question of no account."

"But it's the questions of no account that are always the most interesting."

"Oh, no, this isn't interesting."

"But ask it, and let me judge."

"No, I'll ask another. Don't you think fair women are always much more beautiful than dark ones?"

"Why, no—not always."

"But almost always," persisted Janet; "they look so much purer—and whiter— like angels."

"Well, perhaps," said Tom, and Janet became very grave. "But I know one dark woman," he added, " who is more beautiful than any blonde I have ever seen."

The clouds broke into sunshine on Janet's face. "Oh, Tom," she cried, "I know you don't think I'm half so good-looking as Jerroray ! "

" Well, I didn't say that, did I ? "

"Oh, Tom ! "

" I think you're a great deal better-looking than Jerroray, or any other woman I've ever seen," said Tom, fatuously, quite forgetting the contrary opinion he had lately held when living in the direct light of Jerroray's countenance.

"Oh, Tom ! do you really think so ? I thought her the most beautiful person I'd ever seen, and I know I can't compare to her, but I do like to have you think so ! "

"And you a college girl," said Tom. "Women are all alike."

" Now tell me the other reasons why you tried to fall in love with Jerroray," demanded Janet, becoming practical again.

"Oh, I hoped you'd forget that," said Tom. " Well, I thought she'd be very pleasant and easy to live with, so easy and good-tempered and jolly—all the things you just said about her."

" And is that all? "

" I think so," said Tom, mendaciously.

" Tom, you're not telling the truth—there's something else."

" But I don't wish to say it."

" So I perceive, but you needn't try to evade me."

" Well, it was simply that if I married her, she—you see, she's not been brought up in luxury—she wouldn't want—I mean she'd not mind—— "

" Now, Tom, you must tell me the plain truth. If we can't be openly honest with each other we'd better dissolve partnership at once. Besides, I know what you were going to say—that if you married Jerroray you'd not need to slave yourself to death keeping up an expensive establishment, with lots of servants and horses and expensive gowns for your wife."

" Jerroray is very fond of good clothes," observed Tom.

" But wasn't that it? "

" Possibly—something like it."

" Well. I've been thinking about that, too, ever since what you said to me that night about hating your business. And—and I've come to a conclusion."

" Break it to me," said Tom, cheerfully.
" I can bear it."

" That's what I've been meaning to do
every day since we were married, only there
hasn't been time. This is it. You're not
to go back into the business."

Tom started. " How do you propose to
live?" he asked, after a moment. " Can
you use that costume for a dinner gown—
and dine on air?"

" No," said Janet; " but all the same
it doesn't seem necessary to me to sell our
lives in order to exist in luxury—or rather,
to sell your life. I have thought it all out in
these weeks since we parted. I saw first
how selfish and unsympathetic I was to you
during our engagement, and I regretted it
bitterly. And then I realized suddenly how
much sacrifice I had expected of you throughout our life, and how little I expected of
myself. Most women feel the same and do
the same, but it really isn't our fault so
much as the fault of the way in which
we are brought up. But I made up my
mind that when I had won you back I
wasn't going to have you sell your life
to pay for the money to buy my luxuries,
that we would share our life equally, its

hardships and its joys, and have one equal rule for each.''

'' Well ? '' said Tom.   What was happening seemed to him a miracle, and one more proof that in their mutual divination he and Janet were made for each other.

'' It seemed to me that it was the question of the highway robber over again—and that was before I knew anything about highway robbers—' Your money or your life ? '   The world asks everybody that question, and we can all choose, but almost everybody chooses money.   You and I, Tom, will choose our life, and let the money go.   You shall never go back to that prison of an office.''

Tom was almost too much moved to speak, but after a few minutes he managed to inquire, quite coolly, '' How do you propose to work it practically ? ''

'' Well,'' said Janet, '' luckily I've a little money of my own, from grandfather's estate.   But if I hadn't I should go to work, too, just like you, and earn as much as I could, to go into the common fund, until we could both stop work and begin to enjoy life together, or, rather, until we could begin to do the work we should each really choose to do. Of course there are fortunate people who have that from the start; lawyers are often bound up in their work and would rather do it than anything else in the world, and doctors sometimes feel the same way, and some teachers, and literary men and artists of course. And I'm told that some business men really like their business, though that seems impossible. But most men have to do drudgery that they don't like, hard work that they can't put their hearts into, merely to pay the yearly expenses of living. And as their money increases the expenses of their families increase, and they have to keep on in the treadmill, working harder and harder, with never any stop, never any time to do what they would really like to do, until they are old men, and life comes to an end. And all this while their wives and daughters, dressed in expensive and stylish gowns, are attending fashionable meetings to assert the rights of women and lament over the cruel limitations and wrongs which men put upon them. What I say is let them do their duties first, their share of the work, and talk about their rights afterward. So if you work, I shall work, too, only it must be work that our hearts are in. But I think we might have and enjoy our life for a while and let the money go. I can get along without it if you can. I've got $1,500 a year to live on—how much have you?''

'' Well, I suppose I've saved—in spite of myself—something between thirty and forty thousand dollars,'' said Tom. '' Call it roughly $1,500 a year, too—that would only make $3,000 in all. Could you keep house on that, even? You certainly couldn't have horses, or furniture, or gowns, or——''

'' I don't want any of those things, and I don't want to keep house,'' interrupted Janet. '' I don't want to ' settle down.' I hate settled people and I'm never going to settle myself. Three thousand dollars a year is plenty of money to live very comfortably on in Europe. We can do as we please and dress as we please. We can become masters of all the great languages—French, German, and Italian at least—in the most delightful way in the world, reading their greatest writers, their Goethes and Dantes and Molières, on the very ground where they wrote. We can see the great pictures, and live in the shadows of the most beautiful buildings in the world. We can know charming people, artists, musicians, and writers, living simply but surrounded with beautiful things. And we can live as they do, and every day of life will be perfect, and we shall be growing all the time, and learning, and shall have so many things to enjoy that we can be spendthrifts of enjoyment, and yet always have more than enough left, because it is something that increases trebly with use. Whereas if you stayed in the business, Tom, we should give up all these things for money. We should have a fine house in town, and another in the country, and lots of servants and quantities of clothes, and give fine dinners, and be fat, and prosperous, and stupid, and bored to death. . . . Ah, no, Tom, money costs too much. You and I can't afford to be rich. We will live instead.''

MRS. BURNETT'S
NOVELS AND STORIES

" Mrs. Burnett's characters are as veritable as Thackeray's."—Richard Henry Stoddard.

A Lady of Quality .	$1.50	**Vagabondia.** A Love Story	$1.25
His Grace of Osmonde. Sequel to "A Lady of Quality"	1.50	**Surly Tim, and Other Stories**	1 25
That Lass o' Lowrie's Illustrated . .	1.25	**Earlier Stories.** *First and Second Series.* Each . . .	1.25
Haworth's. Illustrated	1.25	**The One I Knew the Best of All.** A Memory of the Mind of a Child. Illustrated .	2.00
Through One Administration	1.50		
Louisiana	1.25	**The Pretty Sister of José.** Illustrated .	1.00
A Fair Barbarian .	1.25		

MRS. BURNETT'S FAMOUS JUVENILES

New Uniform Edition, each 12mo,
with illustrations by Birch, $1.25

Little Lord Fauntleroy. Over 200,000 copies sold.
Two Little Pilgrims' Progress. A Story of the City Beautiful.
Sara Crewe, Or, What Happened at Miss Minchin's;
Little Saint Elizabeth, and Other Stories.
Piccino, and Other Child Stories.
Giovanni and the Other. Children Who Have Made Stories

For sale by all booksellers; published by

CHARLES SCRIBNER'S SONS
153-157 FIFTH AVENUE   NEW YORK

STEVENSON'S WORKS

Strange Case of Dr. Jekyll and Mr. Hyde $1.00

Fables 1.00

The Vailima Letters. With Portrait. 2 vols. 2.25

The Ebb-Tide . . . 1.25

The Amateur Emigrant 1.25

The following 12mo volumes in uniform binding :

St. Ives. The Adventures of a French Prisoner in England. $1.50

In the South Seas. With Map 1.50

Weir of Hermiston . 1.50

Poems and Ballads. With Portrait . . 1.50

Kidnapped. Being Memoirs of the Adventures of David Balfour in the year 1751. Illustrated . 1.50

David Balfour. Being Memoirs of his Adventures at Home and Abroad . . . 1.50

Treasure Island. With Map 1.00

The Wrecker. *With Lloyd Osbourne*. With 12 full-page illustrations 1.50

The Master of Ballantrae : A Winter's Tale. Illustrated . 1.50

Prince Otto. A Romance $1.00

The Merry Men, and Other Tales . . . 1.25

The Black Arrow. A Tale of the Two Roses. Illustrated . 1.25

New Arabian Nights 1.25

The Dynamiter. More New Arabian Nights 1.25

Island Nights' Entertainments. Illustrated 1.25

The Wrong Box . . 1.25

Across the Plains. With other Memories and Essays . . . 1.25

An Inland Voyage. With Frontispiece . 1.00

Travels with a Donkey in the Cevennes 1.00

The Silverado Squatters. With Frontispiece 1.00

Familiar Studies of Men and Books . 1.25

Virginibus Puerisque, and Other Papers . 1.25

Memories and Portraits 1.25

A Foot-Note to History. Eight Years of Trouble in Samoa 1.50

Memoir of Fleeming Jenkin 1.25

The foregoing 25 vols., 12mo, in a box, . . 32.00

*** *For particulars concerning* THE THISTLE EDITION *of the Complete Works of* ROBERT LOUIS STEVENSON, *sold only by subscription, send for Circular.*

For sale by all booksellers : published by

CHARLES SCRIBNER'S SONS
153-157 FIFTH AVENUE   NEW YORK

FRANK R. STOCKTON'S NOVELS AND STORIES

" There is no more thoroughly entertaining writer before the public to-day than Mr. Stockton."

—*Boston* Globe.

The Girl at Cobhurst $1.50

A Story-teller's Pack. Illustrated . 1.50

Mrs. Cliff's Yacht. Illustrated. . . . 1.50

The Adventures of Capt. Horn . . . 1.50

A Chosen Few. Short Stories. *Cameo Edition.* Portrait . . 1.25

Pomona's Travels. Illustrated 1.50

Rudder Grange. With over 100 illustrations by FROST 1.50

The Watchmaker's Wife, and Other Stories 1.25

The Late Mrs. Null . 1.25

Rudder Grange . . 1.25

The Rudder Grangers Abroad, and Other Stories . . 1.25

The Lady or the Tiger, and Other Stories . 1.25

The Christmas Wreck, and Other Stories 1.25

The Bee-Man of Orn, and Other Fanciful Tales $1.25

Amos Kilbright: His Adscititious Experiences. With other Stories 1.25

Ardis Claverden . . 1.50

Personally Conducted. Illustrated by PENNELL and others 2.00

The Clocks of Rondaine, and Other Stories. Illustrated 1.50

The Floating Prince, and Other Fairy Tales. Illustrated 1.50

Roundabout Rambles in Lands of Fact and Fancy. Illustrated 1.50

Tales Out of School. 300 illustrations . . 1.50

A Jolly Fellowship. Illustrated 1.50

The Story of Viteau. With illustrations by BIRCH 1.50

The Ting-a-Ling Tales. Illustrated 1.00

For sale by all booksellers; published by

CHARLES SCRIBNER'S SONS
153-157 FIFTH AVENUE   NEW YORK

...BY...

THOMAS NELSON PAGE

" Mr. Page's heroines are so delightfully sweet and attractive that no one can help falling in love with them."—Chicago Times-Herald.

Red Rock. A Chronicle of Reconstruction. Illustrated $1.50
Pastime Stories. Illustrated 1.25
In Ole Virginia. Marse Chan, and Other Stories . 1.25.
The Burial of the Guns 1.25
On Newfound River : A Story 1.00
Elsket, and Other Stories 1.00
The Old South. Essays Social and Political . 1.25
New Uniform Edition of the above seven vols., in a box 8.00

The Old Gentleman of the Black Stock. [*Ivory Series*] . . . $ 75
Social Life in Old Virginia Before the War. With Illustrations 1.50
Marse Chan. A Tale of Old Virginia. Illustrated by SMEDLEY 1.00
Meh Lady. A Story of the War. Illustrated by REINHART 1.00
Polly. A Christmas Recollection. Illustrated by CASTAIGNE 1.00

Unc' Edinburg. A Plantation Echo. Illustrated by CLINEDINST $1.00
"Befo' de War." Echoes of Negro Dialect. By A. C. GORDON and THOMAS NELSON PAGE . . . 1.00
Among the Camps, or Young People's Stories of the War. Illustrated 1.50
Two Little Confederates. Illustrated . 1.50

For sale by all booksellers ; published by

CHARLES SCRIBNER'S SONS
153-157 FIFTH AVENUE   NEW YORK

BOOKS BY
GEORGE W. CABLE

" There are few living American writers who can reproduce for us more perfectly than Mr. Cable does, the speech, the manners, the whole social atmosphere of a remote time and a peculiar people."
—*New York* Tribune.

John March, Southerner. $1.50

Bonaventure. A Prose Pastoral of Acadian Louisiana   1.25

Dr. Sevier 1.25

The Grandissimes. A Story of Creole Life . .   1.25

Old Creole Days 1.25

A New Edition of Mr. Cable's Romances comprising the above 5 vols., printed on deckle-edge paper, gilt top, and bound in sateen with full gilt design, now ready, $1.50 per volume. The set in a box . . .   7.50

Strong Hearts 1.25

Strange True Stories of Louisiana. With illustrations and fac-simile reproductions . .   1.25

Madame Delphine 75

The Creoles of Louisiana. Illustrated from drawings by PENNELL 2.50

The Silent South, together with the Freedman's Case in Equity and the Convict Lease System. *Revised and Enlarged Edition.* With portrait .   1.00

For sale by all booksellers ; published by

CHARLES SCRIBNER'S SONS
153-157 FIFTH AVENUE   NEW YORK

HAROLD FREDERIC'S NOVELS

"*The Scribners have in press a new uniform edition of novels and short stories by Mr. Harold Frederic. This is a well-deserved tribute to the abilities of a writer whose worth was recognized by discerning critics long before* 'The Damnation of Theron Ware' *occasioned something of a furor.*"
—*New York* Tribune.

In the Valley	$1.50
Seth's Brother's Wife	1.50
The Lawton Girl	1.50
In the Sixties	1.50

The above four volumes are issued in a handsome uniform binding, gilt top, deckle edges, etc.

Marsena, and Other Stories . . .	$1.00
The Copperhead	1.00
In the Valley. *Illustrated Edition.* With 16 full-page illustrations by HOWARD PYLE	1.50

"*Mr. Frederic's stories of the wartime ('In the Sixties') are constructed thoughtfully and written admirably. They are full of feeling.*"
—*New York* Evening Post.

For sale by all booksellers : published by

CHARLES SCRIBNER'S SONS
153-157 FIFTH AVENUE   NEW YORK

BOOKS BY
RICHARD HARDING DAVIS

"Mr. Davis has vigorous ideals; he is in love with strength and cleanness, with 'grit' and resource, with heroism and courage in men: with beauty and frankness, with freshness and youth in women; and liking these qualities, he also likes writing about them. . . . Mr. Davis has the dramatic gift — he carries you along with him. One need not wish for a better story of action than the 'Soldiers of Fortune.'" — London Academy.

The Cuban and Porto Rican Campaigns
Illustrated from photographs and drawings by eye-witnesses $1.50

The King's Jackal. Illustrated by C. D. GIBSON 1.25

Soldiers of Fortune. Illustrated by C. D. GIBSON 1.50

Cinderella, and Other Stories . . 1.00

Gallegher, and Other Stories . . 1.00

Stories for Boys. Illustrated . . . 1.00

For sale by all booksellers: published by

CHARLES SCRIBNER'S SONS
153-157 FIFTH AVENUE   NEW YORK

BOOKS BY J. M. BARRIE

" Those who know a piece of life when they find it, and who care for the ultimate charm of a bit of pure literature, will read and re-read Mr. Barrie's masterpieces."—Hamilton W. Mabie.

Sentimental Tommy. The Story of His Boyhood. Illustrated by WILLIAM HATH-
ERELL $1.50

Margaret Ogilvy. By Her Son. With etched portrait 1.25

A Window in Thrums. *Cameo Edition.* With an etched frontispiece . . . 1.25

Auld Licht Idylls. *Cameo Edition.* With an etched portrait 1.25

*** *For particulars concerning* THE THISTLE EDITION *of the Complete Works of J. M. Barrie, sold only by subscription, send for circular.*

For sale by all booksellers : published by

CHARLES SCRIBNER'S SONS

153-157 FIFTH AVENUE   NEW YORK

NOVELS AND STORIES
BY
E. W. HORNUNG

"*Mr. Hornung has certainly earned the right to be called the Bret Harte of Australia.*"
—*Boston* Herald.

"*The machinery of Mr. Hornung's fiction, once in motion, is productive of capital and vivid story-telling — stories that hold the interest steadily and never halt for lack of quickening incident and lively adventure.*"—Literature.

The Amateur Cracksman . .	$1.25
Some Persons Unknown .	1.25
Young Blood . . .	1.25
My Lord Duke . . .	1.25
The Rogue's March. A Romance . .	1.50
A Bride from the Bush. [*Ivory Series.*]	.75
Irralie's Bushranger. A Story of Australian Adventure. [*Ivory Series.*] .	.75

For sale by all booksellers : published by

CHARLES SCRIBNER'S SONS
153-157 FIFTH AVENUE   NEW YORK

NOVELS AND STORIES BY "Q"

(A. T. QUILLER-COUCH)

"*Of all the short-story writers, we are inclined, in many respects, to give Mr. A. T. Quiller-Couch the first position.*"—*New York* Times.

"*He is highly esteemed as among the most imaginative and poetic of the late English novelists.*"
—*Philadelphia* Public Ledger.

The Splendid Spur. Being Memoirs of the Adventures of Mr. John Marvel, a servant of His Late Majesty King Charles I., in the years 1642-43. . . . . **\$1.25**

I Saw Three Ships, and Other Winter Tales . 1.25

Dead Man's Rock. A Romance 1.25

The Delectable Duchy. Stories, Studies and Sketches 1.25

The Blue Pavilions. 1.25

Noughts and Crosses. Stories, Studies and Sketches 1.25

Wandering Heath. Stories, Studies and Sketches 1.25

Adventures in Criticism 1.25

The Astonishing History of Troy Town . . 1.25

The above nine volumes are issued in a new uniform edition. The Set, 9 vols., in a box **\$11.00**

Ia. A Love Story. [*Ivory Series*] 75

For sale by all booksellers: published by

CHARLES SCRIBNER'S SONS

153-157 FIFTH AVENUE NEW YORK

www.ingramcontent.com/pod-product-compliance
Lightning Source LLC
Chambersburg PA
CBHW030916270326
41929CB00008B/723